Leadership Traits
Winning Strategies of 50 World
Class Leaders

(And How YOU Can Develop These Traits)

Sati Achath

ISBN: 13: 978-1530867592
ISBN 10: 1530867592

Contents

4. Leaders Are Self-disciplined

Arnold Schwarzenegger - Hollywood actor
Warren Buffett - American business magnate, investor, and philanthropist
David Beckham - British soccer player

5. Leaders Believe in Themselves

Steve Jobs - Co-founder of Apple Computers
Mary Kay Ash - Founder of Mary Kay Cosmetics Inc
Bill Gates - Co-founder of Microsoft
Richard Branson - Founder of Virgin Atlantic airway and 200 other companies

6. Leaders Are Proactive

Theodore (Teddy) Roosevelt - 26th president of the United States
Andrew Carnegie - American industrialist and steel tycoon
Dr. Gilbert Bukenya - Former vice president of Uganda
Salman Khan - Founder of Khan Academy
Oommen Chandy - Chief Minister of Kerala, India
V.J. Kurian - Indian bureaucrat

7. Leaders Have a Positive Attitude

Thomas Edison - Inventor
Nelson Mandela - Former president of South Africa
Chuck Huggins - Former president and CEO of See's Candies
Fred Smith - Founder of FedEx

8. Leaders Are Persistent

President Abraham Lincoln - 16th president of the United States
Henry Ford - Founder of the Ford Motor Company
R.H. Macy - Founder of Macy's department store
Winston Churchill - Former prime minister of the United

Kingdom)

Colonel Harland Sanders - Founder of Kentucky Fried Chicken-KFC

Sam Walton - Founder of Walmart

Ralph Lauren - American fashion designer

Tommy Hilfiger - Creator of the Tommy Hilfiger and Tommy brand clothing lines

9. Leaders Are Early Risers

Pope Francis - Reigning pope of the Catholic Church

Narendra Modi - Prime Minister of India

Tim Cook - CEO of Apple

Robert Iger - CEO of The Walt Disney Company

Al Sharpton – American Baptist, civil rights activist

Margaret Thatcher - Former prime minister of United Kingdom

Thomas Jefferson – American Founding Father

10. Leaders Pursue Excellence

Charlie Chaplin - Comedic British actor

Vince Lombardi - American football coach

Ray Kroc - Built McDonald's into the most successful fast food operation in the world

President Bill Clinton - 42nd president of the United States

Ratan Tata - Indian industrialist and businessman

PREFACE

W ho is a leader? In simple terms, a leader is someone who inspires or influences a group to move towards a goal. I believe that for persons to be effective leaders, they need to develop certain essential character traits inside out that will help them to lead effectively. Before starting to influence other people, a leader needs first to learn how to influence oneself. As leadership guru John C. Maxwell remarked, "Your character qualities activate and empower your leadership ability – or stand in the way of your success. Leaders are effective because of who they are on the inside. To go to the highest level of leadership, you must develop these character qualities from the inside out."

We often admire and adore the leadership styles of world class leaders like President John F. Kennedy, Dr. Martin Luther King, Mahatma Gandhi, and Mother Teresa. But we seldom look into their inherent and innate personal traits which helped them become great leaders. Before they started leading others, they had already empowered themselves with these unique traits within.

So what are those character traits demonstrated by world-class leaders? For this book, I selected ten character traits which are important for a person to be an effective leader. After selecting those ten personal traits, I focused my attention on identifying those leaders who became highly successful mainly because they predominantly possessed one particular trait. Based on my extensive research, I chose 50 world-class leaders who have been categorized under one particular character trait. Their personal traits and stories featured in this book are truly inspiring.

HOW TO MAKE THE BEST USE OF THIS BOOK

I strongly believe that by assimilating the essence of these ten leadership traits and implementing the characteristics under each trait, you will be enabled to unleash your potential. After reading this book cover to cover once to get an overall idea of the book, you should then use it as a guidebook to learn and implement the practical traits demonstrated by these successful leaders. Pay close attention to "Common Characteristics" and "You Too Can Develop," sections, as they will guide you to form an action plan to develop these traits. Write down in a notebook those points you think are very important for you and what actions you should take in order to integrate them into daily life. Also, periodically review what you have put into action and what you have learned from each chapter.

IMPLEMENT WHAT YOU LEARN FROM THIS BOOK

The ten traits and their characteristics discussed in this book are not rocket science! With determination and dedication, you will easily be able to implement all of them in your day-to-day life. Once you master these great traits, you will be in a different league altogether. In brief, armed with these traits, you will be on your way to becoming a highly effective leader, perhaps as much as all the 50 world-class leaders featured in this book.

One
Leaders are Dreamers

"Is it not better to aim my spear at the moon and strike only an eagle than to aim my spear at the eagle and strike only to hit a rock?" - Og Mandino

"The future belongs to those who believe in the beauty of their dreams." - *Eleanor Roosevelt*

"Where there is no vision, the people perish". -Proverbs 29:18

Leaders are dreamers. It will not be an exaggeration to say that all their major achievements and accomplishments start with their dreams. As Napolean Hill has said, "All achievement and all earthly riches have their beginnings in an idea or a dream."

I am sure you will agree with Les Brown when he says, "Go after your dream with a sense of entitlement. You know that you have the power to achieve it and that you deserve it. Be willing to get up into life's face, grab it by the collar and say, 'Give it UP! It's my dream.'"

In this chapter, you will read amazing and inspiring stories of Walt Disney, Marc Zuckerberg, Jeff Bezos, and others who dared to dream and, consequently, achieved a high level of success in their lives. Not only that, but some of their dreams even created a significant impact on human lives. Had they not dared to dream, today, we wouldn't be enjoying and reaping the benefits of their powerful dreams.

Common Traits of Dreamers

- They dream big. They do not limit their vision, and they are not satisfied with small dreams. They know that the effort and energy needed to create a big dream is the same as creating a small dream.

- They brainstorm on what they would like to achieve, and then write down their dreams. Since all those dreams cannot be achieved at the same time, they prioritize their dreams. They decide whether these dreams should be achieved within a definite time frame or simply during their lifetime.

- They visualize. Leaders are effective visualizers; they make a mental picture of what they want to achieve and feel the experience of living through the dream. This visualization motivates them to pursue and work hard to turn their dreams into a reality.

- They undertake even uninteresting tasks. They are willing to undertake tasks that do not interest or excite them when they realize that such tasks would contribute to fulfilling their dreams.

- They seize opportunities. They are prepared to take advantage of an opportunity when it knocks.

- They prepare action plans for converting their dreams into achievable goals.

- They have absolute faith in their dreams.

Walt Disney

(Creator of Disneyland)

Walt Disney was an American film producer, director, screenwriter, cartoonist, and entrepreneur. He holds the record for winning the most Academy Awards (twenty-six awards, including four honorary awards). He was also nominated for an Academy Award sixty-four times.

Disney believed in dreaming big, pursuing those dreams, and transforming them into realities. According to Disney's oldest grandson, Chris Miller, Disney "had big dreams and goals, and he persevered until he achieved them. His life teaches all of us to believe in our dreams, to be daring in the pursuit of our goals, and to never back away from a challenge."

Disney dreamed of an amusement park where adults and children could have fun together. His inspiration came from watching his daughters, Diane and Sharon, ride the merry-go-round together at Griffith Park in Los Angeles. He wanted this park, which he referred to as Disneyland, to be the "happiest place on Earth." He envisioned people visiting Disneyland, "finding happiness there, then going out and widening the circle of happiness around the world."

After developing the initial concept, Disney visited many parks around the world for ideas and inspiration. However, his grand vision encountered skepticism and doubts, and every amusement park operator he talked to said it would fail. He also found it difficult to get financial supporters for the project, which was slated to cost $5 million (and eventually would cost $17 million). To overcome these challenges and materialize his dream, Disney used his life savings and sold and borrowed against all his assets. He finally managed to gather $800,000 to purchase one hundred sixty acres of land for Disneyland in Anaheim, California.

Construction of the park began on July 16, 1954. Disney worked day and night at the site and personally directed construction activities. Exactly one year and one day later, Disneyland was opened on July 17, 1955, featuring twenty attractions. At the dedication ceremony that day, Disney said, "To all who come to this happy place: Welcome. Disneyland is your land. Here, age relives fond memories of the past, and here youth may savor the challenge and promise of the future. Disneyland is dedicated to the ideals, the dreams, and the hard facts that have created America, with the hope that it will be a source of joy and inspiration to all the world."

One hundred seventy thousand people visited Disneyland in the first week, and over one million visitors went there in the first two months. As of 2013, over six hundred fifty million people have visited Disneyland so far.

Disney's other dream project, Disney World, in Lake Buena Vista, Florida, was developed in the 1960s. Unfortunately, Disney died in December 1966 from lung cancer, before the construction started. Disney World was opened on October 1, 1971. Over a sprawling twenty-five thousand acres of land, Disney World currently houses twenty-four themed resorts, four theme parks, two water parks, and several additional recreational and entertainment venues. It is the most visited entertainment complex in the world, attracting 52.5 million people annually.

Walt Disney is a classic example of someone who dared to dream big and had the vision, courage, and motivation to overcome cynicism and predictions of failure, and finally succeeded in transforming his dream into a reality.

Mark Zuckerberg
(Cofounder of Facebook)

Mark Zuckerberg, cofounder of Facebook, was born on May 16, 1982, in White Plains, New York. He was very interested in computers as a child and developed excellent skills in programming. When he was twelve, he created a messaging program called ZuckNet. His father used ZuckNet in his dental office, which enabled the receptionist to inform the dentist when a patient entered his office. Zuckerberg's family also used ZuckNet to communicate with each other inside the house. While he was in high school, he built a music player called Synapse Media Player that used artificial intelligence to learn the user's listening habits. Even though AOL and Microsoft were interested in buying this program, Zuckerberg declined their offers.

As an undergraduate student at Harvard University, Zuckerberg developed a program called Course Match with the intention of helping students choose their classes based on the course selections of other students. Very soon he also developed Facemash, which let students compare photos and select the best-looking person.

After developing these successful programs, Zuckerberg started dreaming of creating a program where people were able to connect with each other, socialize, and share information for free. He was convinced that people were interested in keeping up friendships and knowing what their friends were doing. On February 4, 2004, Zuckerberg, along with four friends, launched Facebook from his Harvard University dormitory room. To begin with, Facebook was only meant for Harvard students, but Zuckerberg decided to expand it to other schools including Stanford, Columbia, Cornell, and Yale universities.

To devote all his time to Facebook and focus on creating innovations and adding new features, Zuckerberg dropped out of Harvard in June 2004 and moved the company to Palo Alto, California. By December 2004 one million people were using Facebook, and by December 2005 the number of users had increased to 5.5 million. As of March 2014, 1.28 billion people are using Facebook.

What started as a medium to help Harvard students communicate with each other, Zuckerberg's dream project, Facebook, has grown into a mammoth social network. He has revolutionized the way millions of people around the world keep in touch and share information instantly and freely. Time magazine named Zuckerberg Person of the Year in 2010 and among the one hundred wealthiest and most influential people in the world.

Jeff Bezos

(Founder of Amazon.com)

Jeff Bezos, founder of Amazon.com, was born on January 12, 1964, in Albuquerque, New Mexico. Right from his childhood, Bezos displayed a keen interest in computers and electrical gadgets. This interest took Bezos to Princeton University, where he studied computer science and electrical engineering. After graduation from Princeton in 1986, Bezos started working on Wall Street. In 1990 he moved to the investment firm D. E. Shaw & Co. in New York City, where he soon became a senior vice president at age twenty-six. While working at D. E. Shaw, Bezos's research on Internet opportunities showed that the Internet's growth rate at that time was 2,300 percent a year. Impressed with the exponential growth of the Internet, Bezos made a list of twenty products that could be successfully sold online.

Bezos decided that he would try selling books online because of the large worldwide demand for literature, low price points for books, and huge number of titles available in print. In 1994 Bezos resigned from his lucrative job at D. E. Shaw and moved to Seattle, Washington, with the dream of launching a successful online bookstore. Bezos's decision to pursue his dream was based on his concept of "regret minimization framework," according to which he wanted to reduce the number of regrets he would have at age eighty. Bezos said, "I knew that if I failed I wouldn't regret that, but I knew the one thing I might regret is not ever having tried. I knew that that would haunt me every day, and so, when I thought about it that way, it was an incredibly easy decision."

In Seattle Bezos and his employees set up an office in his garage and began developing the software for an online bookstore. On July 16, 1995, he launched Amazon.com, named after the South American river. In the first thirty days,

Amazon sold books in the United States and over forty-five countries, and in the first two months, it was selling $20,000 in books each week. By December 1995 sales had jumped to $510,000, and in 1997 Amazon's revenue crossed $15 million.

In 1998 Bezos diversified Amazon's sales to CDs, DVDs, MP3 downloads, electronics, toys, clothes, and other products through major retail partnerships. In 2007 Amazon launched the Kindle, an electronic book reader that allows consumers to download books and read them at their convenience. In September 2011 Amazon released the Kindle Fire, a tablet that allows consumers to watch shows, browse the web, and play games. The Kindle Fire sold out on the first day. In 2012 Amazon's revenue was $61.09 billion. As of September 2013, Amazon had about one hundred ten thousand employees.

With his vision, foresight, and dream, Bezos revolutionized online shopping as well as the book publishing industry. He was named 1999 Man of the Year by Time magazine. In 2008 Bezos was named one of America's best leaders by the U.S. News & World Report. In 2014 Bezos's net worth was $32.3 billion.

Sergey Brin and Larry Page

(Cofounders of Google)

Sergey Brin, cofounder of Google, was born on August 21, 1973, in Moscow, Russia. Brin immigrated to the United States with his family when he was six years old. He received his undergraduate degree in mathematics and computer science from the University of Maryland, College Park. After graduation he moved to Stanford University to do a PhD in computer science. At Stanford, Brin's specific interest was in the field of data mining, which means extracting meaningful patterns from mountains of information.

Larry Page, the other cofounder of Google, was born on March 26, 1973, in East Lansing, Michigan. After earning a bachelor's degree in computer engineering from the University of Michigan, he moved to Stanford University to pursue a PhD in computer science.

Brin and Page met in 1995 during an orientation for new PhD students at Stanford. After spending some time together, they "became intellectual soul-mates and close friends." In 1996 they began working on how to harness information on the World Wide Web, and they dreamed of creating a search engine that would "organize the world's information and make it universally accessible and useful."

Brin and Page originally called their new search engine BackRub because their system checked back links to estimate the importance of a website. Later they changed the name of the search engine to Google, which was a misspelling of the word googol, the number one followed by one hundred zeros. This name was chosen to indicate that the search engine aimed to provide large quantities of information available on the web. Initially, Google ran under Stanford University's website, and its domain names were Google.Stanford.edu and Z.Stanford.edu. Subsequently, Brin and Page gathered funds from family, friends, and faculty members to buy some servers and started operating from a friend's garage in Menlo Park, California. In September 1998 Google was incorporated as a company, and since then it has become the world's most popular search engine, receiving more than two hundred million queries every day.

Google's annual revenue for 2012 was $50 billion. As of September 2013, Google has seventy offices in more than forty countries. According to Forbes magazine, in 2013 Brin was the twenty-first-richest person in the world, with a personal wealth of $24.4 billion, and Page was the twentieth-richest person in the world, with a personal wealth of $24.9 billion.

Google's employees enjoy several perks, including three free meals a day, free food delivery for new parents, and full on-site medical care. For this reason, Fortune magazine has ranked Google as the number one place to work in the United States.

Jack Dorsey
(Cocreator of Twitter)

Twitter, which has revolutionized the way people communicate, was created because of Jack Dorsey's dream. Born on November 19, 1976, in St. Louis, Missouri, Dorsey became interested in computers and communications at a very young age. In particular, he was fascinated with dispatch routing for coordinating taxis, delivery vans, couriers, and emergency vehicles that needed real-time communication. When he was fifteen years old, Dorsey developed software for dispatching logistics that is still used by many taxi companies.

After studying computer science at New York University for a few semesters, Dorsey dropped out of college and moved to Oakland, California. In 2000 he started a company selling dispatch software online to dispatch couriers, taxis, and emergency services personnel. During his work he witnessed thousands of workers in the field constantly updating where they were and what they were doing. This experience gave him the idea of simplifying the design for general usage by the public. Dorsey soon began to dream of launching a program where people could easily share what they were doing with their friends in real time.

Dorsey then started a company called Obvious with Evan Williams and Biz Stone. Obvious was later renamed Twitter. Within two weeks, Dorsey had created a website where users could post short instant messages, known as tweets, of one hundred forty characters or less. On March 21, 2006, Dorsey posted the first tweet: "Just setting up my twitter."

Even though Twitter was initially looked down upon, it soon became a powerful worldwide social networking phenomenon. In 2008 the US presidential candidates,

Barack Obama and John McCain, used Twitter to update their supporters while on the campaign trail. Likewise, in 2009 when the Iranian government blocked text messaging after the presidential elections, Twitter users in Iran started giving updates on the political events there. By 2014 Twitter had more than five hundred million users who tweeted about three hundred forty million times per day.

In November 2013 after Twitter's initial public offering (IPO), the company's share price increased from $26 to $250 on the first day of trading. On that day itself, Dorsey's 23.4 million shares made him a billionaire.

Dorsey was recognized as one of Time magazine's 100 Most Influential People in the World and was named one of MIT Technology Review's 35 Innovators Under 35 in 2008. In 2012 the Wall Street Journal honored him with the Innovator of the Year Award for technology.

Verghese Kurien

(Revolutionized milk production in India)

Verghese Kurien is best known as the "Father of the White Revolution" or the "Milkman of India." Kurien was born in November 26, 1921, in Kerala, India. He earned bachelor's degree in physics from Loyola College, Madras and bachelor's degree in mechanical engineering from College of Engineering, Guindy, Madras in India. He earned a master of science degree in mechanical engineering from Michigan State University in 1948.

Kurien's dream was to use cooperatives to take India from being a milk-deficient nation to being the largest milk producer in the world. Kurien was able to achieve his dream through a unique program called Operation Flood, launched in 1970. The bedrock of Operation Flood was village milk-producers' cooperatives. These cooperatives procured milk from village milk producers directly and, after processing it, supplied milk directly to urban markets, thereby avoiding middlemen and malpractice. Modern management and technology were made available to milk producers by the cooperatives. This model helped milk producers direct their own development and placed control of their resources in their own hands. In turn, those cooperatives became powerful agents of social change by empowering women and alleviating poverty for millions of people in rural India.

Because of Operation Flood, India's annual milk production increased from 23.3 million tons in 1968–69 to 110 million tons in 2006–07. Operation Flood made India the largest milk producer in the world, surpassing the United States. The success of Operation Flood has resulted in the replication of this model for other commodities, including fruits and vegetables.

Kurien's outstanding contributions earned him numerous honors and awards, including the Carnegie Foundation's Wateler Peace Prize, the World Food Prize, the Padma Vibhushan (India's second-highest civilian award); and the Ramon Magsaysay Award for Community Leadership.

You Too Can Fulfill Your Dreams

- Brainstorm on the things you would like to achieve in your lifetime.
- Write down as many dreams as possible that you would like to achieve.
- Prioritize your dreams according to your preference. Decide whether you want to achieve them within a definite time period or during your lifetime.
- Be willing to undertake even those tasks that may not appear interesting or exciting if you think those tasks will help you achieve your dreams.
- Read both your list of dreams and your action plan at least a few times every week.

Two
Leaders Set Goals

"The greater danger for most of us is not that our aim is too high and we miss it, but that it is too low and we reach it." – Michelangelo

"If you want to be happy, set a goal that commands your thoughts, liberates your energy and inspires your hopes." –Andrew Carnegie

"Leadership is the capacity to translate vision into reality." - Warren Bennis

It is an indisputable fact that none of us will start a journey without knowing where we are going. This analogy is very much relevant in our life's journey as well. Then why is it that very few people set goals in their lives? Leaders, on the other hand, know that it is vital to establish goals in their quest for success in life. As Earl Nightingale eloquently stated, "People with goals succeed because they know where they are going."

Achievements of incredible goals set by President John F. Kennedy, Mustafa Kemal Ataturk, and Lee Kuan Yew in this chapter are truly inspiring. I am sure that their success stories will inspire you to set your own goals and motivate you to achieve them.

Common Traits of Goal Setters

- They prepare a list of their desires and goals. They write down a list of all the desires they want to fulfill. Some of them even make a list that has more than one hundred desires on it

- They write down SMART goals. Leaders write SMART goals: specific, measurable, achievable, realistic, and time bound goals. Once the goals are identified, they classify these goals into short-term goals (up to one year), midterm goals (up to three years), and long-term goals (beyond three years). They set their priorities on these goals according to their importance.

- They visualize. In their minds they visualize each goal as if they have already accomplished it, and then they feel the experience of enjoying that goal. This visualizing process increases their motivation to work for actually achieving that goal. For example, Jack Nicklaus, a legend in golf, has acknowledged that he employs visualization. In his own words, "I never hit a shot, not even in practice, without having a very sharp, in-focus picture of it in my head. It's like a color movie."

- They create a comprehensive to-do list for each day. At the end of the day, either before leaving the office or going to bed, they prepare a to-do list of important tasks to be done the next day, so when they wake up they will have clear ideas on how to get their tasks done faster and better. Every morning they look at the to-do list and work on the top-priority task until it is completed. After completing the first task they move on to the second task, and so on. If there are some tasks that don't get done that day, they move them to the next day's list.

- They continually improve their skills in key areas. Most of them spend at least one hour every day reading materials related to key areas in their life.

- They focus on their strengths. They identify their strengths and focus on strengthening them further.

President John F. Kennedy

(Thirty-fifth president of the United States)

John Fitzgerald Kennedy (May 29, 1917–November 22, 1963) was the thirty-fifth president of the United States from January 1961 until his assassination in November 1963. Five months after becoming president, on May 25, 1961, President Kennedy stated that Congress of the United States should "commit itself to achieving the goal, before this decade is out, of landing a man on the moon and returning him safely to the earth. Kennedy urged the United States to work diligently to lead the achievements of space travel because "in many ways [it] may hold the key to our future on earth."

There were a few political facts that affected Kennedy's decision. First, Kennedy was under great pressure to have the United States "catch up to and overtake the Soviet Union in the 'space race." "Second, the failed military invasion of Cuba at the Bay of Pigs in April 1961 also put pressure on Kennedy. Third, Kennedy was keen to announce a program that the United States had a strong chance at achieving before the Soviet Union.

This challenging decision called for tremendous human efforts and financial commitment to transform Kennedy's goal into a reality by 1969. Projects Mercury, Gemini, and Apollo were designed for this purpose. The lofty goal was finally achieved eight years later, before the end of the decade, when Apollo 11 commander Neil Armstrong set his foot on the moon's surface on July 20, 1969.

Mustafa Kemal Atatürk

(Founder and first president of the Republic of Turkey)

Mustafa Kemal Atatürk, the founder and first president of the Republic of Turkey (born on May 19, 1881), was a charismatic leader and a towering personality. He led the Turkish national liberation struggle, put an end to the antiquated Ottoman dynasty, and created the Republic of Turkey in 1923.

As the president Atatürk's goal was to modernize Turkey. To achieve this goal, he initiated a large number of political, economic, and cultural reforms to transform the former Ottoman Empire into a modern, secular, democratic nation-state, based on the rule of law. He and other intellectuals looked into all contemporary solutions to modernize the state, and most of the systems developed by Western governments were used as models while developing country-specific reforms. They wanted to promote human rights and enlightenment, especially for the poor and neglected people in rural areas.

As the president of Turkey for fifteen years from January 1923 until his death in 1938, Atatürk introduced a broad range of swift and sweeping reforms in various domains such as political, social, legal, economic, and cultural spheres. These included replacing the Arabic alphabets with the Latin alphabet, introducing the Gregorian calendar, and encouraging contemporary lifestyle, modern society, and a fully independent secular country. Atatürk also industrialized the nation, established state-owned factories, and built a railway network. Further, he enacted several laws to establish legal equality between the sexes. For example, he removed women's veiling laws and gave women the right to vote. He also introduced the process of parliamentary and participatory democracy.

Through these extraordinary and innovative administrative measures, Atatürk succeeded in restoring his people's pride in their nation and bringing Turkey into the modern world.

Atatürk's Turkey dedicated itself to the sovereignty of the national will and the creation of, as Atatürk said, "The state of the people." In 1933 Atatürk said, "I look to the world with an open heart full of pure feelings and friendship."

Atatürk was regarded as a great leader who stood for the principles of humanism and the vision of a united humanity. Glorious tributes have been paid to him by world statesmen including Winston Churchill, Franklin D. Roosevelt, Jawaharlal Nehru, Charles de Gaulle, and John F. Kennedy.

Atatürk died on November 10, 1938, at the age of fifty-seven.

Lee Kuan Yew

(First prime minister of Singapore)

Lee Kuan Yew (born on September 16, 1923) is regarded as the founding father of modern Singapore. He was the first prime minister to govern the country for three decades, from June 1959 to November 1990. When he became the prime minister, Lee's goal was to make Singapore a financial and industrial powerhouse, despite its lack of natural resources.

After Singapore separated from Malaysia and became an independent country in 1965, Lee ruled Singapore with great authority, discipline, and firmness. He maintained religious tolerance and racial harmony, and focused on developing the economy. Even though Singapore had a small population, limited area, and lack of natural resources, Lee considered that Singapore's only natural resource was its people and their strong work ethic.

In his first term as prime minister, Lee introduced a five-year plan, with emphasis on urban renewal, construction of new public housing, greater rights for women, educational reform, and industrialization. He also spearheaded a program to transform Singapore into a major exporter of finished goods and worked on attracting foreign direct investment. With his charismatic and inspiring leadership, Lee ran the country efficiently and ensured a high standard of living and prosperity for its citizens. By the 1980s Singapore had a per capita income second only to Japan's in Eastern Asia.

As an able administrator, Lee succeeded in transforming Singapore from a relatively unknown country to a first-world Asian tiger. Lee's achievements were so impressive and magnificent that they earned plaudits from many world leaders. According to former US president George H. W. Bush, Lee is "one of the brightest and most effective world leaders that I have ever known." Likewise, former US president Bill Clinton called Lee a "remarkable leader and statesman."

You Too Can Develop Goals

• Think of all you desire to achieve in your life, and write down your goals. For example, your desire could be changing your personality or behavior, improving your self-confidence, losing weight, becoming a voracious reader, becoming a novelist, learning musical instruments, or learning new languages.

• Write down your goals as SMART goals—specific, measurable, achievable, realistic, and time bound. They should be in the form of positive affirmations.

• Write down your goals in first person and present tense.

• Visualize your goals vividly so it is easier to feel as if you are living through the experience. As Lou Tice says in his book Small Talk, "Visualize your goal close enough so you can see yourself in it."

• Think of the many benefits you can enjoy upon the realization of your goals, and write them down.

• Prepare an action plan for accomplishing each goal. Identify and write down potential obstacles and hurdles standing in your way. Think of ways you can overcome these obstacles and hurdles, and write them down. Identify additional skills, knowledge, and resources you will need. Also, prepare a list of people whose help you may need.

• Identify your strengths and focus on further strengthening them. Give more time, attention, energy, and resources to build on your strengths.

- Create a comprehensive to-do list for each day. At the end of each day, either before leaving the office or going to bed, prepare a to-do list of important tasks to be done the next day. Every morning look at the to-do list and work on the highest-priority task until it is completed. After completing that task, move on to the second task, and so on. If there are some tasks that don't get done that day, move them to the next day's list.
- Be discreet in discussing your goals. Share them only with those you implicitly trust and who will encourage you.
- Monitor the progress of your goals a few times each week. Determine whether you are close to achieving your goals or not, and take remedial actions if needed.

Three
Leaders Are Committed

"If I don't practice for a month, the audience can tell the difference. If I don't practice for a week, my wife can tell the difference. If I don't practice for a day I can tell the difference." –Fritz Kreister

"Commitment: Doing the things that others won't do, in order to have the things that others won't have. " - Dr. Creflo Dollar

"Before you are a leader, success is all about growing yourself. When you become a leader, success is all about growing others." — Jack Welch

Leaders are committed wholeheartedly to achieving their goals. Because of their passion and commitment, they have a burning desire to achieve what they have determined to achieve. They possess a deep level of determination and an unflinching dedication. They also recognize that staying committed is extremely important to achieving their goals. Their passion enables them to outperform those who possess great skills but have no commitment. They also exhibit enthusiasm, which is one of the most important ingredients for success.

Because of a strong commitment to their chosen endeavors, leaders are willing to face physical hardships, troubles, failures, rejections, and humiliation. Lives of Mother Teresa, Mahatma Gandhi, Dr. Martin Luther King, Jr., and other leaders show that they will undergo any amount of hardships and sacrifices to fulfill their commitment.

Common Traits of Committed People

- They have determination and dedication. They possess a deep level of determination and an unflinching dedication to achieving their goals. They give their undivided attention in order to perform consistently at high standards. They recognize that staying committed to achieving their goals and fulfilling their dreams is important. Their passion for achieving goals makes them dedicated, committed, productive, and effective people.

- They take whatever actions are needed. Once they decide on their goals, they work on whatever actions are needed to achieve them. They have the self-discipline to be consistent and stay committed to their decisions.

- They are not deterred by failures and setbacks. The fire within fuels them with energy and dynamism to pursue their goals, even when they face failures, defeats, and setbacks.

- They enhance their skills. For personal excellence and tapping their potential, they are engaged in lifelong learning. They upgrade their existing skills and learn new skills on a continual basis. As part of continual learning, they invariably spare at least one hour every day to read on subjects or topics related to their fields. They educate themselves to do those things they are passionate about. Further, they also associate with passionate people for inspiration. They emulate the good qualities of role models in their fields and do their best to be like them.

- They are enthusiastic. They exhibit enthusiasm, which is one of the most important ingredients for success. Their enthusiasm is infectious, and as Shiv Khera says in his book You Can Win, their "enthusiasm inspires confidence, raises morale, builds loyalty and is priceless." Their commitment motivates them to spend more time on what they enjoy doing and enables them to get more work done in less time.

- They are willing to pay the price. Irrespective of the time it would take or the obstacles along the way, they are prepared to pay the price for achieving their goals.

- They overcome their fears. Because of a strong commitment to their chosen endeavors, they overcome their fear of failure, rejection, humiliation, and the unknown. Since they overcome these fears through self-discipline, they are more confident to pursue their desires and goals.

Mother Teresa

(Founder of the order of the Missionaries of Charity)

Mother Teresa was born Agnes Gonxha Bojaxhiu on August 26, 1910, in Skopje, Republic of Macedonia (Skope at that time was called Uskiep, and it was located in the Ottoman Empire). Her parents were of Albanian descent. As a child Agnes was fascinated by the lives of missionaries and their service in India. Around age twelve she was convinced that she should pursue a religious life and become a missionary to spread the love of Christ. At age eighteen Agnes left her home in Skopje and joined the Sisters of Loreto, an Irish community of nuns who were doing missionary work in India. After learning English for about a year in Ireland, she arrived in India in 1929 and began her novitiate in Darjeeling, near the Himalayas. Agnes took her initial vows as a nun on May 24, 1931. At that time Agnes opted to be named Teresa.

Mother Theresa taught at St. Mary's High School in Calcutta, India, from 1931 to 1948. During this period, she was deeply disturbed by the suffering and poverty she saw in Calcutta. This emotional disturbance prompted her to seek permission from her supervisors to leave the convent school and commit herself to helping the poorest of the poor in the slums of Calcutta.

In 1948 Mother Theresa started her missionary work. She became an Indian citizen, received basic medical training at Holy Family Hospital in Patna, Bihar, and began working in the slums of Calcutta. There, she started an open-air school for children. Soon, volunteer workers joined her, and financial help started pouring in. This enabled her to start tending to the needs of the destitute and starving people.

In October 1950 Mother Theresa received permission from

the Vatican to start her own order, the Missionaries of Charity. The goal of the Missionaries of Charity, in her own words, was to care for "the hungry, the naked, the homeless, the crippled, the blind, the lepers, all those people who feel unwanted, unloved, uncared for throughout society, people that have become a burden to the society and are shunned by everyone."

Although it started as a small order with thirteen members in Calcutta, by 1997 the Missionaries of Charity had grown to more than four thousand sisters running orphanages and AIDS hospices and undertaking relief work in the wake of natural catastrophes for refugees all over the world. By 2007 the Missionaries of Charity had almost four hundred fifty brothers and five thousand sisters worldwide, operating six hundred missions, schools, and shelters in one hundred twenty countries.

Mother Theresa's work was acclaimed around the world, and she was the recipient of many awards and distinctions. In 1979 she was awarded the Nobel Peace Prize "for work undertaken in the struggle to overcome poverty and distress in the world, which also constitute a threat to peace." She received other awards including the Pope John XXIII Peace Prize (1971); India's highest civilian award, Bharat Ratna (1980); and the Balzan Prize (1978).

Mother Theresa died on September 5, 1997, at the age of eighty-seven.

Mahatma Gandhi

(Leader of India's independence movement)

Mohandas Karamchand Gandhi, more commonly known as Mahatma (meaning "great soul") Gandhi, was born on October 2, 1869, in Porbandar, Gujarat, India. It was Gandhi's commitment to nonviolence that became a powerful tool to help India fight against British colonialism and regain its independence.

In 1893 after studying law at the Inner Temple Law College in London, Gandhi went to South Africa and lived there for twenty years. During his life there, Gandhi was appalled by the discrimination against Indians. On a train journey to Pretoria, he was thrown out of a first-class coach and beaten up by a white stagecoach driver when he refused to give up his seat for a white passenger. This bitter incident was a turning point in Gandhi's life, and he soon developed the concept of satyagraha (truth and firmness) or passive resistance, which is a nonviolent way of protesting against injustice.

In 1914 Gandhi returned to India and became involved in India's independence movement. In 1919 he launched a campaign of passive resistance against the passage of the Rowlatt Acts, which gave emergency powers to British authorities for suppressing subversive activities. He backed off when violence broke out and about four hundred Indians attending a meeting at Amristar in Punjab were massacred by British soldiers.

After Gandhi's civil disobedience campaign from 1919 to 1922, he was jailed for sedition for two years. In 1924 Gandhi observed a twenty-one-day fast from his prison cell when India was embroiled in violent Hindu-Muslim riots. In 1930 Gandhi launched a new civil disobedience campaign, known as the "Salt March," against the British government's tax on salt, which affected the poorest Indians. For this campaign Gandhi and his followers marched two hundred miles from Sabarmati Ashram to the Arabian Sea to collect salt in symbolic defiance of the government monopoly. The Salt March soon became a national campaign, and thousands of people went to beaches to pick up loose salt. Indian-made salt was then sold across the country. The British government reacted to this situation with mass arrests, including imprisoning Gandhi without a trial. Realizing that this campaign could not be stopped, the British viceroy Lord Irwin granted limited salt production. Gandhi viewed this decision as the first step on the road to independence.

In 1942 Gandhi asked the British to "quit India" and every Indian to lay down his or her life, if needed, for India's freedom. The government responded again by imprisoning Gandhi for two years. Witnessing that India was on the verge of a violent civil war because of the Hindu-Muslim riots across the country, Britain granted independence to India on August 15, 1947, and created Pakistan as a Muslim country.

To stop the widespread violence between Hindus and Muslims in an independent India, Gandhi once again started a fast on January 13, 1948. Realizing that a frail and aged Gandhi would not be able to withstand a rigorous fast, both Hindu and Muslim leaders agreed to work together to stop the violence and create peace in the country. On this assurance, Gandhi ended his fast after five days. Unfortunately, twelve days after the fast ended, on January 30, 1948, the seventy-eight-year-old Gandhi was shot to death in Delhi by a young Hindu fanatic, Nathuram Godse. (Gandhi had survived five earlier assassination attempts.)

Dr. Martin Luther King Jr.
(Leader in the African American civil rights movement)

Dr. Martin Luther King Jr., a Baptist minister and civil rights activist, was born as Michael King Jr. on January 15, 1929, in Atlanta, Georgia. He adopted the name Martin Luther King Jr. in honor of the German Protestant religious leader Martin Luther. After earning a degree in sociology from Morehouse College in 1948 and a bachelor of divinity degree from Crozer Theological Seminary in 1951, King earned his PhD in systematic theology from Boston University in 1955 at age twenty-six. In 1954 King became a pastor of the Dexter Avenue Baptist Church in Montgomery, Alabama.

For about twelve years, from December 1955 until his assassination on April 4, 1968, King's commitment was to achieve equality for African Americans in the Unites States. As the leader in the civil rights movement, he was inspired by his Christian faith, the teachings of Mahatma Gandhi, and other advocates of nonviolence.

King was the leader of the first nonviolent demonstration, the Montgomery Bus Boycott, to protest the arrest of Rosa Parks when she refused to give up her seat to a white passenger on a Montgomery bus on December 1, 1955. After 382 days of African Americans boycotting Montgomery buses, the US Supreme Court ruled in November 1956 that racial segregation in transportation was unconstitutional.

In January 1957 King, along with sixty ministers and civil rights activists, founded the Southern Christian Leadership Conference (SCLC) for mobilizing the power of black churches and conducting nonviolent protests to promote civil rights reform. The motto of SCLC was "Not one hair of one head of one person should be harmed." In 1963

King led a coalition of civil rights groups to boycott, sit-in, and march to protest the segregation and unfair policies in Birmingham, Georgia, which at the time was considered the "most segregated city in America." Police used brutal force to crush these nonviolent campaigns, and King was arrested on April 12, 1963. The "Letter from Birmingham Jail" King wrote at that time became the civil rights manifesto defending civil disobedience.

On August 28, 1963, King and a number of civil rights and religious groups organized the "March on Washington for Jobs and Freedom." This peaceful political rally, which was attended by over a quarter million people, highlighted injustices that African Americans faced in the United States. King delivered his famous "I Have a Dream" speech at this rally. The "March on Washington" rally is consider instrumental in the passage of the Civil Rights Act of 1964, which made it illegal to discriminate against African Americans or minorities in hiring, education, transportation, or public accommodations. In August 1965 Congress passed the Voting Rights Act, which guaranteed the right to vote for all African Americans. This legislation was the direct result of the march for voting rights campaign led by King from Selma to Montgomery, Alabama.

In 1964 at age thirty-five, King became the youngest person ever to win the Nobel Peace Prize. That same year King was also named Time magazine's Man of the Year. On April 4, 1968, at the young age of thirty-nine, King was assassinated while standing on the balcony of a hotel in Memphis, Tennessee, where he was to lead a protest march to support a sanitation workers' strike.

President Barack Obama

(Forty-fourth president of the United States)

Barack Obama, the forty-fourth president of the United States and the first African American to hold the office, was born on August 4, 1961, in Honolulu, Hawaii. After graduating from Columbia University in 1983 with a bachelor's degree in political science, Obama worked as a community organizer in Chicago. He earned his law degree from Harvard Law School in 1991, and then taught constitutional law at the University of Chicago Law School from 1992 to 2004. After serving three terms in the Illinois senate from 1997 to 2004, he became a US senator in January 2005. Obama was inaugurated as US president on January 20, 2009.

Obama has always been passionate about reforming the US health-care system. He was concerned that millions of US citizens were denied health coverage because of preexisting conditions, that people could be dropped from their health insurance plans when they got sick, and that they could run out of health insurance coverage because of a lifetime limit imposed by their insurance company. Obama was equally disturbed by the fact that 62 percent of people found it difficult or impossible to find affordable coverage and 62 percent of personal bankruptcies had medical-related causes.

As a person who genuinely cares for the well-being of ordinary American people, Obama was frustrated with the inequities and injustice prevailing in the US health-care system. To rectify this frustrating situation in the country, Obama made health-care reform a top priority in his 2008 presidential campaign. He made it his commitment to expand health insurance coverage to cover the uninsured, cap premium increases, and allow people to retain their coverage when they leave or change jobs.

After becoming president, Obama signed the Patient Protection and Affordable Care Act (ACA) into law on March 23, 2010. The predominant features of ACA are as follows:

- Insurance companies can no longer discriminate against Americans by denying coverage because of preexisting conditions.

- It's now illegal for health insurance companies to arbitrarily cancel health insurance just because a person gets sick.

- Health plans are required to cover key essential benefits like hospitalizations, mental health services, and prescription drugs.

- Insurance companies can no longer impose annual or lifetime limits on a plan's essential health benefits.

- Women can no longer be charged higher premiums just because they are women.

- Young adults can stay on their parent's health insurance plan until the age of twenty-six—a change that has already allowed more than 3.1 million young adults to receive health coverage.

Through ACA Obama has succeeded in fulfilling his commitment to strengthening consumers' rights, providing affordable health insurance coverage, and providing greater access to medical care for all Americans.

You Too Can Be Committed

- Visualize the benefits of achieving your goals—this visualizing process will enable you to be committed, enthusiastic, and passionate about achieving your goals.

- Be enthusiastic and cheerful on all occasions. This powerful trait will enable you to overcome all obstacles and challenges and stay committed to your cause.

- Be passionate and enthusiastic in your actions and behavior.

- Be in the company of motivated people. Their enthusiasm and positive attitude will inspire you to be motivated and committed.

- Make positive affirmations, such as stating that you are deeply committed and will achieve your goals at any cost.

- Keep reading and learning new things for fresh ideas, which will keep you committed and motivated.

- Monitor your progress and see if you will need to make any changes in your actions to remain committed.

Four
Leaders Are Self-Disciplined

"The first requisite for success is to apply your physical and mental energies to one problem incessantly without growing weary." –Thomas Edison

"Self-discipline is the ability to do what you should do, when you should do it, whether you feel like it or not." - Elbert Hubbard

"My own definition of leadership is this: The capacity and the will to rally men and women to a common purpose and the character which inspires confidence." - General Montgomery

Leaders will agree that self-discipline is an important quality that enables them to achieve their goals. This great quality has transformed the lives of many of them and made them highly successful in many areas, including academics, business, literature, sports, and all other spheres. They also know that while lack of discipline leads to failures, sufferings, frustration, and underachievement, self-discipline will open for them doors of opportunities to achieve success in any sphere of life. Being aware of the tremendous benefits of self-discipline, leaders will maintain it as an integral part their daily routine.

In this chapter, you will be impressed with the high level of self-discipline on the part of Arnold Schwarzenegger, Warren Buffet, and David Beckham. You will notice that it was their relentless practice of self-discipline that mainly enabled them to achieve their goals and become highly successful in life.

Common Traits of Self-Disciplined Leaders

- They are self-motivated people who don't need to be reminded or instructed to do their work. They chart their daily routines and plans and are consistent in maintaining them.

- They possess self-control, which enables them to manage their thoughts, behaviors, actions, activities, and speech. They are in charge of their emotions, desires, and actions, and they don't surrender to undesirable inclinations, temptations, or urges. They do things that are appropriate and consistent with their long-term goals and objectives.

- They are well-organized people. Since they are fully aware that being disorganized saps time and energy, they are organized in all their chores and daily activities. Their daily routines are well planned. For instance, they plan their days the night before and prepare a to-do list for the next day. They set priorities and execute each task with complete focus and concentration. For them, being organized also means clearing clutter and keeping their home, work, schedule, and finances in order.

- They avoid procrastination. They keep everything they will need for a job ready and available. They use various tactics to avoid procrastination: One is the "do it now" approach in which they complete a task as early as possible. Second is the "finish it now" approach in which they finish a task or project completely, rather than putting aside some part of it for later. Third is to do the unpleasant, difficult, or complex tasks first and then move on to more enjoyable and simple tasks.

- They have the ability to say "no" when the situation demands, both to themselves and to others.

- They do not make excuses. To achieve their goals, self-disciplined people do what they should do when they should do it, without making any excuses.

- They are cool, calm, and composed while finding solutions to problems and dealing with crises.

- They focus their attention on important matters and do not let trivial things distract them.

- They learn from mistakes. They believe in the adage "When you lose, don't lose the lesson." They learn from their mistakes, failures, defeats, and setbacks. For them, failures are stepping-stones to success, and they accept defeats gracefully and move forward.

- They have good time-management skills. Their conscious use of time helps them in their self-discipline process. They direct their choices, actions, and behaviors in such a way that they are more productive and effective each day.

- They take care of their health. They eat healthy food and exercise regularly for physical fitness and to stay healthy.

Five
Leaders Believe
in Themselves

"The mind is the limit. As long as the mind can envision the fact that you can do something, you can do it - as long as you really believe it 100%." -Arnold Schwarzenegger

"If you think you CAN ... or if you think you CAN'T ... you're right!" - Henry Ford

"Leadership is lifting a person's vision to high sights, the raising of a person's performance to a higher standard, the building of a personality beyond its normal limitations." - Peter Drucker

Leaders believe strongly in their abilities, skills, and vision and are confident that they will ultimately succeed in meeting their goals and fulfilling their dreams. They are not discouraged or deterred by criticisms or failures. They will agree with the words of Napolean Hill: "You can be anything you want to be, if only you believe with sufficient conviction and act in accordance with your faith; for whatever the mind can conceive and believe, the mind can achieve."

The power of believing in yourself is vividly demonstrated by the superb achievements of Bill Gates, Steve Jobs, Richard Branson, and other leaders mentioned in this chapter. By emulating this predominant quality of these role models, you too will be on your path to a highly successful life.

Common Traits of Leaders Who Believe in Themselves

- They have faith in themselves. They have faith in their ability to face life's challenges, obstacles, and adversities, and to overcome them with triumph.

- They are not distracted. They are so confident in their beliefs that they are not distracted by negative assessments, criticisms, and failures.

- They do self-talk. They make positive affirmations such as "I am successful," "I have tremendous willpower," and "I am feeling great." When they make such positive affirmations, their brains store these affirmations in the subconscious and act upon them.

- They are creative. They come up with new ideas and ways to find solutions to problems.

- They manage their thoughts, emotions, anger, and temper very well and remain focused on achieving their goals.

Steve Jobs

(Cofounder of Apple Computers)

Steve Jobs, entrepreneur, creative genius, and visionary, was the cofounder of Apple Computers. Born on February 24, 1955, in San Francisco, California, Jobs was given up for adoption soon after birth by his biological parents.

During his life, Jobs faced series of failures, setbacks, and obstacles, but he was able to overcome them because of his tremendous belief in himself. For example, after high school graduation in 1972, Jobs enrolled at Reed College. Reed was an expensive college, and Jobs's adopted parents could not afford to pay for his education, so he dropped out of college after six months. During his brief stay at Reed, he used to sleep on the floor of friends' rooms because he did not have a dormitory room. To meet his expenses, he collected empty Coke bottles and occasionally got free meals at the local Hare Krishna temple.

In 1976 at the age of twenty-one, Jobs and his friend Steve Wozniack started Apple Computers in Jobs's parents' garage. The company was named Apple because of Jobs's nostalgia for his summer job picking apples. After a few years of successful performance, the company's sales declined in 1982 because of competition from IBM's new computers. In 1985 Jobs was fired from the company he founded by its CEO, John Sculley, following a dispute over control of Apple. Instead of accepting defeat or getting depressed, Jobs's belief in himself prevailed. In a speech given to Stanford University students in 2005, Jobs said that getting fired from Apple was the best thing that could have happened to him. "The heaviness of being successful was replaced by the lightness of being a beginner again, less sure about everything. It freed me to enter one of the most creative periods of my life." Jobs also said, "I'm pretty sure none of this would have happened if I hadn't been fired from Apple. It was awful tasting medicine, but I guess the patient needed it."

In 1985 Jobs founded a hardware and software company called NeXT Inc. In the first year, the company didn't have any product, and it ran out of money. Jobs didn't get frustrated and sought venture capital. Fortunately, billionaire Ross Perot invested heavily in NeXT. However, NeXT Inc. was not very successful; the struggling company was bought by Apple Computers in 1997 for $429 million, and Jobs was appointed Apple's CEO.

Once Jobs was back at Apple, he revitalized the company and introduced innovative products such as the iPod, iPad, and iTunes. Jobs's effective branding campaigns and sophisticated designs made Apple a highly successful company. Apple has been ranked first on Fortune magazine's list of America's Most Admired Companies.

The graphic company Pixar that Jobs bought from Lucas Films in 1986 was also a phenomenal success. Computer-animated films such as Toy Story, A Bug's Life, and Finding Nemo made Jobs a multibillionaire. Jobs passed away on October 5, 2011, due to pancreatic cancer.

Mary Kay Ash

(Founder of Mary Kay Cosmetics, Inc.)

Mary Kay Ash (born May 12, 1918, in Hot Wells, Texas) was an American businesswoman and entrepreneur. She played an important role in the advancement of women entrepreneurs in the United States. Ash's immense success as an entrepreneur can be attributed to her belief in herself as well as her charisma, optimism, and positive attitude.

While working at Stanley Home Products, a direct-sales company offering housewares and cleaning supplies, Ash was frustrated to see that the glass ceiling kept many women from reaching top positions in the male-dominated corporate world. Even though she was a top sales producer, she found that men who were less competent and efficient were promoted over her. In Ash's next job at World Gift Co., her suggestions were often ignored by her male colleagues with the comment, "Oh, Mary Kay, you're thinking just like a woman." In 1962 when a man she had trained was appointed as her supervisor and paid twice her salary, Ash quit her job at World Gift Co.

After going through a series of bad experiences in the traditional workplace, Ash wrote a book to help women avoid the pitfalls she had encountered during her career. She prepared two lists, with the first list narrating her negative experiences and the second list explaining the qualities that would constitute an ideal "dream company" for workingwomen. While reviewing the second list, Ash thought, "Why [am I] theorizing about a dream company? Why don't [I] just start one?" Thus, in 1963 at the age of forty-five, Ash decided to start her own cosmetics business using her five-thousand-dollar life savings.

Ash purchased the recipes for skin lotions from a tanning

store and recruited a sales force consisting of nine friends. Unfortunately, one month before the company was scheduled to open, Ash's husband, who had been assisting her on legal and financial aspects, died of a heart attack. Under the belief that Ash would not succeed without her husband's help, her lawyer and accountant advised her to drop her plans. But Ash's belief in herself prevailed, and she ignored the advice of her lawyer and accountant. On September 13, 1963, Ash opened Mary Kay Cosmetics in Dallas.

Because of Ash's innovative and unique strategies in direct-sales business, within the first four months, Mary Kay sold $34,000 worth of products. Within one year, the sales had increased to $800,000, and the sales force had grown to more than three thousand consultants. Ash rewarded top-performing consultants with diamond jewelry, five-star vacations, and even pink Cadillac cars. By 1983 the company's sales had reached $324 million, and by 1993 sales had risen to $1 billion and it had become the largest direct seller of skin-care products in the United States. In 2001 Mary Kay Cosmetics had more than eight hundred thousand representatives in thirty-seven countries with total annual sales of over $2 billion. In 2011 Mary Kay was the sixth-largest direct sales company in the world, with net sales of $2.9 billion. The company was featured three times in Fortune magazine's 100 Best Companies to Work for in the United States.

Numerous business leaders, politicians, academicians, and authors have recognized Ash's belief in herself, as well as her brilliance and determination. She received several prestigious awards during her lifetime and many more following her death on November 22, 2001. She was called one of America's 25 Most Influential Women by The

World Almanac and Book of Facts (1985), inducted into the National Business Hall of Fame by Fortune magazine (1996), named the most outstanding woman in business in the twentieth century by Lifetime Television (1999); and named one of PBS's and the Wharton School of Business's 25 Most Influential Business Leaders of the Last 25 Years (2004).

Bill Gates

(Cofounder of Microsoft)

Bill Gates, the man behind the personal computer revolution, believed in himself beyond doubt. Born on October 28, 1955, at the age of thirteen, Gates wrote his first computer program on a General Electric computer in BASIC, which allowed users to play games against the computer. Because of his keen interest in programming, his school excused Gates from math classes so he could pursue his passion. At age seventeen, Gates, along with his friend Paul Allen, wrote a program called Traf-O-Data to make traffic counters based on the Intel 8008 processor. After joining Harvard University in 1973, Gates spent a lot of time using Harvard's computers. In 1975 when the MITS Altair 8800 was released based on the Intel 8080 CPU, Gates and Allen saw this as an opportunity to launch their own computer software company. Because of Gates's belief in himself, he was confident that his company would be a success, and he took the risk of dropping out of Harvard. After noticing his confidence and belief in himself, Gates's parents supported his decision to drop out of Harvard and start a company. In 1975 Allen and Gates started their own company Micro-Soft, based in Albuquerque, New Mexico. Within one year they dropped the hyphen, and on November 26, 1976, they registered Microsoft in New Mexico.

Microsoft succeeded in developing programming-language software for various systems. In January 1979 Microsoft moved from Albuquerque to Bellevue in Washington State. In the first five years of Microsoft's existence, Gates reviewed every line of the code the company shipped, and, if needed, rewrote them. In 1980 Microsoft made a deal with IBM to produce its operating systems. By 1982 the company had sold software worth $32 million. Over the next few years, Microsoft grew exponentially.

In 1987 Gates was listed as a billionaire in Forbes magazine's four hundred richest people in America, just a few days before he turned thirty-two. As the world's youngest self-made billionaire, Gates was worth $1.25 billion. In 2004, 2005, and 2006, Time magazine named Gates as one of the 100 People Who Most Influenced the 20th Century. In 2006 he was placed eighth in the list of Heroes of Our Time. In 2012 Forbes ranked Gates as the fourth most powerful person in the world. Gates was made an honorary Knight Commander of the Order of the British Empire (KBE) by Queen Elizabeth II in 2005.

Richard Branson

(Founder of Virgin Atlantic airway and two hundred other companies)

Richard Branson (born on July 18, 1950, in Surrey, England) is the founder of Virgin group, which holds more than two hundred companies in more than thirty countries, including Virgin Atlantic airway, Virgin Records, and Virgin Galactic.

As a child, Branson struggled with dyslexia. He dropped out of high school at the age of sixteen. Even though he knew that he was a poor student, he did not let his academic failures prevent him from tapping into his hidden potential. Instead, he believed in himself, his ability to connect with others, and his knack for business. After dropping out of school in 1966, Branson published a magazine called Student. This magazine, run by students, for students, sold $8,000 worth of advertising in its first edition. The first issue of Student distributed fifty thousand copies for free, and the cost of releasing the first issue was recovered from the advertising revenue.

In 1970 Branson set up an audio record mail-order business under the name Virgin. He advertised the most popular records in Student magazine and sold the records at a cheaper price compared to other outlets.

The name Virgin was suggested by one of Branson's employees because they were all new to business. Due to the overwhelming success of this business, in 1972 Branson set up a chain of record stores named Virgin Records. The same year he purchased a mansion in London and set up a recording studio. He leased out time for artists to use the recording facilities of the studio. This venture also became hugely successful, as Branson was offering quality products at less cost.

Branson started Virgin Atlantic airways in 1984, Virgin Mobile in 1999, and Virgin Australia in 2000. In 1996 he acquired Eurobelgian Airlines and renamed it Virgin Express. Virgin America was started in 2007. In 2004 Branson opened a new space-tourism company called Virgin Galactic, which plans to make space flights open to the public, with tickets priced at $200,000.

In the Forbes 2012 list of billionaires, Branson was ranked as the sixth-richest citizen of the United Kingdom, with an estimated net worth of $4.6 billion. Branson's highly successful entrepreneurship is proof that, even more than academic achievements, believing in himself was a critical factor in his life. According to Branson, "My interest in life comes from setting myself huge, apparently unachievable challenges and trying to rise above them...from the perspective of wanting to live life to the full, I felt that I had to attempt it."

You Too Can Believe in Yourself

- Develop confidence in your abilities, skills, and talents, and have faith in your ability to face challenges, obstacles, and adversities and overcome them successfully.

- Don't get discouraged or distracted by negative comments, criticisms, failures, or setbacks.

- Keep a positive attitude, and be optimistic that eventually you will overcome obstacles and successfully achieve your desires and goals.

- Think of creative ideas to find solutions to your problems.

SATI ACHATH

Six
Leaders Are Proactive

"I know of no more encouraging fact than the unquestionable ability of man to elevate his life by conscious endeavor." – Henry David Thoreau

"People are always blaming their circumstances for what they are. I don't believe in circumstances. The people who get on in this world are the people who get up and look for the circumstances they want, and if they can't find them, make them." - George Bernard Shaw

"The best executive is the one who has sense enough to pick good men to do what he wants done, and self-restraint enough to keep from meddling with them while they do it." - Theodore Roosevelt

Leaders who are proactive are highly self-motivated. Without any external influence, they take the initiative to do things they need to do to achieve their goals. They always explore opportunities on their own and take actions to make the best use of those opportunities. In the words of Stephen R. Covey, "Proactive people can carry their own weather with them. Whether it rains or shines makes no difference to them. They are value driven; and if their value is to produce good quality work, it isn't a function of whether the weather is conducive to it or not."

The proactive quality of President Theodore Roosevelt, Andrew Carnegie, and other successful people proves beyond doubt the powerful impact it can have in achieving success in life.

Common Traits of Proactive Leaders

- They are self-motivated. Without any external influence, they take the initiative to do things they need to do to achieve their goals.

- They always explore opportunities on their own and take actions to make the best use of those opportunities.

- They anticipate problems before they happen and take proactive efforts to prevent them.

- They don't complain. Instead of bemoaning their adverse circumstances and challenges or waiting for others to rescue them, they take actions to overcome challenges

- They take initiative to acquire skills and knowledge that will help them find solutions to problems. They also take whatever actions are needed to get a job done.

- They are willing to take risks. They make things happen even if there is a high chance of making mistakes or failing.

Theodore (Teddy) Roosevelt

(Twenty-sixth president of the United States)

Theodore Roosevelt, the twenty-sixth president of the United States (1901–1909) (born on October 27, 1858), was known for his exuberant personality, multifarious interests, and "cowboy persona." He was the youngest US president ever, at the age of forty-two, and also the first of only three sitting presidents to have won the Nobel Peace Prize.

Roosevelt is regarded as one of the most proactive US presidents of the twentieth century. He said that "there is nothing brilliant or outstanding in my record, except perhaps this one thing. I do the things that I believe ought to be done. And when I make up my mind to do a thing, I act." Some of the proactive actions Roosevelt took during his administration include involvement in the completion of the Panama Canal, helping to negotiate an end to the Russo-Japanese War (for which he won a Nobel Peace Prize in 1906), supporting desegregation and women's suffrage.

In addition to his political achievements, Roosevelt published more than twenty-five books on a wide range of subjects including history, biology, geography, and philosophy. He also published a biography and an autobiography, including The Winning of the West in four volumes. He is consistently rated by scholars as one of the greatest US presidents along with George Washington, Thomas Jefferson, and Abraham Lincoln. Roosevelt has pride of place atop Mount Rushmore.

Andrew Carnegie

(American industrialist and steel tycoon)

The rags-to-riches story of Andrew Carnegie is a testament to the benefit of being proactive. Industrialist, businessman, and major philanthropist, Carnegie was born on November 25, 1835, in Dunfermline, Scotland. His father, William Carnegie, was a handloom weaver, and the family struggled in poverty. In 1849 William Carnegie and his family moved to Pennsylvania, seeking a better life. Carnegie, who was thirteen at the time, started working as a bobbin boy, changing spools of thread in a cotton mill in Pittsburg, working twelve hours a day, six days a week, and earning $1.20 a week.

In 1850 Carnegie found a job as a telegraph messenger boy in the Pittsburg office of the Ohio Telegraph Company, earning $2.50 a week. In 1853 he became a telegraph operator at the Pennsylvania Railroad Company with a salary of $4.00 a week. Three years later Carnegie was promoted to superintendent.

Right from his first job at age thirteen, Carnegie kept his eyes open and was always on the lookout for opportunities. He strove to be the best at whatever job he was given. He also realized the importance of education and spent his free time reading books at public libraries and attending night school. Carnegie did not wait for opportunity; instead, he searched for it. He believed that "The first man gets the oyster, the second man gets the shell."

Carnegie's proactive quality was amply demonstrated in his work in the steel industry. One of his great inventions involved the cheap and efficient mass production of steel using the Bessemer process for steelmaking. As a result of this technology, the price of steel dropped considerably, and Bessemer steel was used henceforth for railway lines and girders. Carnegie's next proactive innovation was his vertical integration of all suppliers of raw materials. For each stage of the production process, Carnegie owned whatever was needed, such as raw materials, ships and railroads for transporting goods, and even coalfields to fuel the steel furnaces. Due to Carnegie's innovative and proactive measures, by the late 1880s Carnegie Steel became the largest manufacturer of pig iron, steel rails, and coke in the world, with a capacity to produce about two thousand tons of pig metal per day.

Carnegie's other proactive approach was to identify and hire the right people as his advisors for each job so he could run his business efficiently. He had the knack of getting the right resources so that he could produce the best product.

During his lifetime, Carnegie earned almost $400 million, out of which he donated about $350 million (the equivalent of billions in today's dollars) to universities, libraries, and organizations dedicated to research in science, education, world peace, and other causes. Carnegie used to say that, "It is the mind that makes the body rich. There is no class so pitiably wretched as that which possesses money and nothing else."

Gilbert Bukenya

(Former vice president of Uganda)

Dr. Gilbert Bukenya is a Ugandan physician and politician and was the vice president of Uganda from May 2003 to May 2011. Born in May 1949, Dr. Bukenya got his bachelor of medicine degree from Makerere University School of Medicine in Uganda, his master of science (MSc) degree from the London School of Hygiene & Tropical Medicine, and his PhD from the University of Queensland, Australia. He served as the dean of Makerere University School of Medicine from 1994 to 1996.

In Uganda Dr. Bukenya is well regarded as an outstanding leader who is highly proactive, innovative, and committed to transforming communities. For instance, while many African leaders were reluctant to recognize the growing problem of HIV and AIDS that afflicted the people of their respective countries, Dr. Bukenya took a proactive stance to combatting this malady in Uganda. As the vice president of Uganda, Dr. Bukenya identified upland rice as a major strategic intervention for food security and poverty reduction. The Upland Rice Project is widely acknowledged as the turning point in the growth of Uganda's rice sector. In 2007 Dr. Bukenya received the prestigious US Congressional Gold Medal Award for his poverty alleviation program, Prosperity for All, which specifically targets peasant farmers.

Salman Khan

(Founder of the Khan Academy)

Educator Salman Khan's proactive approach to using the Internet has triggered a revolution in the field of education. Khan, whose father hails from Bangladesh and whose mother hails from India, was born on October 11, 1976, in New Orleans, Louisiana. He graduated with a BS in mathematics and a BS in electrical engineering and computer science from the Massachusetts Institute of Technology. After earning an MBA from the Harvard Business School in 2004, Khan started working as a hedge fund analyst at Connective Capital Management in New York.

In late 2004, Khan began tutoring his cousin Nadia, who lived in Louisiana, in mathematics over the Internet using the Yahoo! program Doodle. When the rest of his family and friends heard about the free tutoring and sought similar help, he filmed the tutorials and posted them on YouTube so that anybody could view them whenever they chose. In 2009 Khan quit his job to devote all his time to the Khan Academy's tutorials.

The Khan Academy is a nonprofit educational organization providing "a free world-class education for anyone anywhere." Its website has thousands of educational resources, including a personalized learning dashboard, over one hundred thousand practice problems, and over six thousand microlectures via video tutorials stored on YouTube. The subjects covered include mathematics, physics, chemistry, biology, astronomy, cosmology, history, medicine, and finance. All the resources are available for free to anyone around the world. As of June 23, 2014, the Khan Academy channel on YouTube has attracted 1.8 million subscribers, and the videos have been viewed over 413 million times. The academy's website has also been translated into twenty-three languages.

The Khan Academy is funded by donations, including funding from the Bill and Melinda Gates Foundation, Google, and the Brazil-based Lemann Foundation. Khan published a book about the Khan Academy called The One World Schoolhouse: Education Reimagined. In 2012 Time magazine named Salman Khan in the list of the 100 Most Influential People in the World. Forbes magazine featured Khan on its cover, with the story about "the $1 trillion opportunity." According to Bill Gates, "Khan's impact on education might truly be incalculable."

Oommen Chandy
(Chief minister of Kerala, India)

Oommen Chandy (born October 31, 1943), the chief minister of Kerala, is a highly proactive person. Soon after becoming the chief minister in August 2011, Chandy launched the Mass Contact Programme with the main aim of combating red tape and bureaucracy in administration. It was aimed at enabling interaction between the people and the government by encouraging people to approach the government directly to address their concerns without delay or corrupt practices.

Under the program, Chandy visits each town and organizes massive events where people can address their queries personally. By going directly to the people and ensuring direct access to decision makers, the program has improved accountability in Kerala. The initiative has reduced the time usually taken to respond to complaints and actions and has fast-tracked problem solving.

Before the Mass Contact Programme was started, there was a low follow-up rate on grievances and complaints from citizens. Characterized by high bureaucracy, Kerala faced efficiency challenges and a very low response rate, which led to a large volume of grievances and complaints. Complaints about government officers were not addressed properly by senior officials, and people had limited options for solutions to their problems with public services. This led to files piling up in various departments and government secretariats, with 1,320,000 files pending in the Kerala Secretariat by mid-2011.

The UNDP appreciated Chandy for his range of proactive and innovative practices in democratic governance for strengthening people's access and participation in human development and governance. The UNDP was impressed by Chandy's innovative approach to ensure transparency and accountability in governance, particularly the web streaming of the entire functioning of the chief minister's office. The Mass Contact Programme, in many ways, is the first of its kind to ensure the right to direct access to government leaders and senior civil servants.

Chandy received the prestigious 2013 United Nations Public Service Award for the category "preventing and combating corruption in the public service." The award was based on the theme "Transformative e-Government and Innovation: Creating a Better Future for All." Globally, the United Nations gives this award to five geographical regions. Chandy's Mass Contact Programme took first prize for the Asia-Pacific region. The award is usually won by an entire department or group of countries, but the 2013 award was won by Chandy alone.

V. J. Kurian

(Indian bureaucrat)

V. J. Kurian, a senior officer in the Indian Administrative Service (IAS), has left impressive and memorable imprints wherever he worked. Belonging to the Kerala cadre of the IAS, Kurian is well-known for qualities such as his proactive approach, strong determination, commitment, persistence, and visionary leadership.

Kurian came to national prominence in India for his outstanding role in building the Cochin International Airport Limited (CIAL), India's first greenfield airport in the private-public partnership. His role is used as a case study on managerial issues related to corporate leadership and ethics. The case study "VJ Kurian & the CIAL Saga" was written by professors Rameshan and Jeyavelu of the Indian Institute of Management (IIM) Kozhikode in Kerala, who remarked that Kurian "was full of ideas, often totally novel. He knew how to implement them through team work and with the confidence of everyone in the organization."

When the National Airports Authority of India (NAAI) and Kerala government did not have the money to construct the airport in Nedumbassery, Kerala, Kurian came up with the idea that the construction could be funded by nonresident Indians (NRIs) who were using international airports like Mumbai to reach Kerala. Very soon, with the overwhelming response from the NRIs and local population, CIAL was able to mobilize the required funding for the construction of the airport. During a six-year period from 1993 to 1999, with his proactive attitude, determination, and decisive leadership, Kurian overcame all the hurdles and obstacles and triumphed to make the CIAL airport a successful venture.

As the Spices Board chairman from 2006 to 2011, Kurian was equally proactive. During this period, he completed many spice parks, research centers, and laboratories for ensuring quality of spices. He also initiated e-trade to enable farmers to earn more income.

You Too Can Be a Proactive Person

- Develop the quality of self-motivation, and take the initiative to do what is needed to achieve your goals.
- Always look for opportunities, and take suitable actions to make the best use of these opportunities.
- Don't be bothered too much about making mistakes or failing while you are taking actions to achieve your goals.
- Be enthusiastic about learning new skills and acquiring knowledge that will help you find solutions to your problems.
- Don't whine over unfavorable circumstances or challenges. Likewise, don't wait for anybody to come rescue you. Instead, take actions to overcome these obstacles.

Seven
Leaders Have Positive Attitudes

"Attitude is the first quality that marks the successful man. If he has a positive attitude and is a positive thinker, who likes challenges and dif¬ficult situations, then he has half his success achieved." - Lowell Peacock

"If you sow negative thoughts, your life will be filled with negative things. If you sow positive thoughts, your life will be cheerful, successful, and positive." - Earl Nightingale

"Men make history and not the other way around. In periods where there is no leadership, society stands still. Progress occurs when courageous, skillful leaders seize the opportunity to change things for the better." - Harry S. Truman

A positive attitude is a valuable quality for a person's success. As William James, psychologist and philosopher, has remarked, "People can alter their lives by altering their attitudes of mind."

The same idea has also been expressed by Jim Rohn when he said, "One of the fundamental things that every person who wants to improve his or her life should work on is his or her attitude. Your attitude determines so much about how you will live your life and how far you will go in life."

Leaders have shown that a positive attitude gives them limitless possibilities and potential for accomplishing what they want. The positive attitudes of Thomas Edison, Nelson Mandela, and others in this chapter are truly mesmerizing as well as energizing.

Common Traits of Leaders with Positive Attitudes

- They are optimists who look at the bright side of any situation and always expect positive results. For them, challenges and setbacks are just passing phases, so when they are faced with challenging situations, they focus on finding solutions to their problems.

- They believe in themselves and their abilities, and they have courage and confidence to overcome challenges and hurdles, which are essential qualities for success.

- They are not afraid of failures or making mistakes. They look upon failures and mistakes as experiences from which they can learn valuable lessons for the future.

- They are fully aware of the dangers of negativity that would drag them down emotionally and physically. They also know that negativity is the destroyer of their success.

- They have pleasing personalities and their positive self-esteem makes them feel good about themselves. They are enthusiastic in their outlooks, enthusiastic toward others' achievements, and do their best to help others.

- They handle stresses very well by balancing time at work with spending time on leisurely activities such as reading, watching TV, or hobbies.

- They are not influenced by negative people, and they avoid being associated with such people.

- They deal directly with people to resolve conflicts. When there is a conflict or a problem with a colleague or a friend, they deal directly with that person to resolve the conflict or problem.

Thomas Edison

(Inventor of the electric light bulb, the phonograph, and many other devices)

Thomas Edison greatly influenced human lives with his inventions, including devices such as the phonograph, kinetograph (motion-picture camera), incandescent electric bulb, and alkaline storage batteries. Dubbed the "wizard of Menlo Park," during his lifetime, Edison had a record 1093 US patents to his name, as well as patents in the United Kingdom, France, and Germany.

Born on February 11, 1847, in Milan, Ohio, Edison had a difficult childhood. Due to a breakout of scarlet fever and a number of ear infections, he had hearing difficulties in both ears, and this malady made him nearly deaf in his adult life. Being a hyperactive child, Edison was considered a difficult student by his teachers; consequently, his mother pulled him from school and taught him at home.

Edison's hallmark quality was positive attitude. He refused to consider anything as a failure or become discouraged by setbacks. He would say, "Every wrong attempt discarded is another step forward." While researching the incandescent light bulb, Edison wrote over forty thousand pages of notes before he invented a bulb that withstood a forty-hour test in his laboratory. He tested more than sixteen hundred materials, including coconut fiber, fishing line, and hair from the beard of one of his friends. Finally in 1870, Edison and his team chose carbonized bamboo as the right material for the filament. When Edison was asked how many times he had failed before inventing the incandescent light bulb, he replied, "I have not failed. I've just found 10,000 ways that won't work." Even after Edison's lab in West Orange, New Jersey, was destroyed in a fire in 1914 and he lost all his assets, he remained positive. He said, "I am 67; but I'm not too old to make a fresh start. All our mistakes are burned up. Thank God we can start anew." Edison reconstructed the lab soon after the accident and worked there for another seventeen years—best of all, within three weeks of the fire, he invented the phonograph!

Edison died on October 18, 1931, at the age of eighty-four, due to complications from diabetes.

Nelson Mandela

(Former president of South Africa)

Nelson Rolihlahla Mandela (born on July 18, 1918, in Mvezo, South Africa) was one of the greatest statesmen of the twentieth century. His life is an inspiration to everyone, especially to those who are oppressed and deprived.

Mandela became actively involved in the antiapartheid movement in his twenties and joined the African National Congress (ANC) in 1942. For twenty years, Mandela was in charge of a campaign of peaceful, nonviolent defiance against the racist policies of the South African government. In 1961 Mandela began to believe that armed struggle was the only way to end apartheid, which was one of the great abominations of the century. Soon, he cofounded Umkhonto We Sizwe, known as MK, an armed wing of the ANC, which believed in sabotage and guerilla war tactics to end the apartheid.

In June 1964 Mandela and seven others were sentenced to life in prison for political offenses, sabotage, and promoting revolution. Mandela was incarcerated on Robben Island for eighteen years from 1964 to 1982. He was isolated from nonpolitical prisoners and imprisoned in a concrete cell that was eight feet by seven feet with a straw mat for sleeping. Mandela contracted tuberculosis during this period, and he was physically and verbally tormented by white prison wardens.

At Robben Island, Mandela had to work in a lime quarry without breaks, and the glare from the sun permanently damaged his eyesight. He was allowed only one visit and one letter every six months, with all mail heavily censored. Newspapers were forbidden, and he was locked on solitary confinement several times for possessing smuggled news clippings. From April 1982 to December 1988, Mandela was incarcerated at Pollsmoor Prison in Capetown, and from December 1988 until he was released in February 2000, he was imprisoned at Victor Verster Prison.

During the twenty-seven years of incarceration under demeaning conditions, Mandela never lost his spirit or hope. Instead, he was full of positive attitude. He had unflinching optimism and faith that one day apartheid would come to an end and racial equality would be established in South Africa. This positive attitude and optimism kept him going. As he had hoped for, soon after he was released from prison, apartheid was abolished in South Africa.

A few examples of Mandela's positive attitude in the face of adverse circumstances are demonstrated by his actions, behavior, and achievements. For instance, while in jail he refused privileges if they were offered to him but not to other prisoners, he was a mentor to his fellow prisoners and encouraged them to use nonviolent resistance for getting better treatment in prison, he studied for his LLB degree at night, and he earned a bachelor of law degree from the University of London through the correspondence program, and wrote his autobiography, Long Walk to Freedom.

Even after he became the president of South Africa in 1994, Mandela retained his positive attitude. He did not hold any bitterness or vindictiveness against his captors or political opponents; instead, he displayed an astonishing capacity for forgiveness and conciliation. He emphasized personal forgiveness and reconciliation and announced that "courageous people do not fear forgiving for the sake of peace." He formed a multiracial Government of National Unity and proclaimed South Africa a "rainbow nation at peace with itself and the world." He reassured South Africa's white population that they were protected and represented in "the rainbow nation." When South Africa hosted the 1995 Rugby World Cup, Mandela urged both blacks and whites to support the predominantly Afrikaner national rugby team.

As Economist magazine remarked, Mandela's "greater achievement, though, was to see the need for reconciliation, to forswear retribution and then to act as midwife to a new, democratic South Africa built on the rule of law. This was something only he could do."

Mandela died at his home in Johannesburg on December 5, 2013.

Chuck Huggins

(Former president and CEO of See's Candies)

Chuck Huggins, who worked with San Francisco's venerable chocolate company See's Candies for fifty-five years, was a warm, outgoing, and gregarious man whose positive attitude won the hearts of his colleagues and anyone who interacted with him. He had a big, easy smile, and he built a reputation for his sincere and genuine interest in people. He remembered their names, took a personal interest in their welfare, and would do his best to be helpful to them.

Chuck was born on March 2, 1925, to American parents in Vancouver, British Columbia, Canada and grew up in Portland, Oregon, USA. After high school graduation, he served in the US military during World War II and later graduated from Kenyon College with a BA in English literature.

In 1951 Chuck joined See's Candies in Los Angeles as a management trainee. Because of his hard work and sincerity, he was soon promoted to manager. In 1972, due to the See family's confidence in Chuck, they relied on him to help sell the firm to Warren Buffet. Chuck impressed Buffett to such an extent that Buffett appointed Chuck as president and CEO of the company and retained him in those positions for the next thirty-four years. "It took me about 15 seconds to realize Chuck was the person for the job," Buffett reportedly said at the time.

As CEO Chuck remained humble and referred to himself as "chief taster," since he was involved in the selection of new candies and retiring those candies that were no longer popular. He is estimated to have sampled three hundred thousand pieces of See's candy during his career and was instrumental in developing the popular Awesome Bars. He also helped save such candies as the Ginger, Marzipan, and Marsh Mints from extinction. Under Chuck's leadership, the company grew to five thousand employees and two hundred stores with sales revenue of more than $300 million.

For those who worked at See's Candies, Chuck was known as a "people person" with a positive attitude who remembered employee's names and details about their families. He was very charming and extremely thoughtful. According to Margaret Pick, author of the book See's Famous Old Time Candies: A Sweet Story, Chuck "was one of those people who would approach everyone with the same respect and demeanor of care. Walking through See's Candies stores with him or through a factory with him, people just lit up when he came in because that level of personal touch and personal care was there. And it was absolutely genuine."

Chuck's positive attitude was also reflected in his personal life. He was a fun guy with a keen interest in jazz music. He was an accomplished drummer and singer, who regularly performed with his good friend Tom Ford in T Ford and the Model A's, a band that played charitable events in the Bay Area and even toured Europe.

A big supporter of education, Chuck worked with various school boards. He was also a benefactor to many wild animal and marine mammal centers. An avid outdoorsman, he was active with the Boy Scouts, which he later felt prepared him for being an army paratrooper during World War II with the 513th Parachute Infantry Regiment, 17th Airborne Division. Chuck's love of animals, conservation, travel, and other activities gave him opportunities to be in touch with people.

Chuck passed away on August 19, 2012, at the age of eighty-seven from a stroke.

Fred Smith

(Founder of FedEx)

Fred Smith is the founder, chairman, president, and CEO of Federal Express (FedEx), the world's first and largest overnight delivery service. He was born on August 11, 1944, in Marks, Mississippi. Fred graduated with a bachelor's degree in economics in 1966 from the prestigious Yale University.

As a senior student at Yale, Smith wrote a paper on his vision for an overnight delivery service in the computerized information age. His professor told him that his concept was interesting, but not feasible. He got a C grade for his paper. Smith was not deterred by his grade or the negative comments about his dream project. Instead, he was positive that his idea would prevail, so he kept it as a secret pet project.

After his graduation from Yale in 1966, Smith served in the US Marine Corps, flying a crop duster during the Vietnam War, and in 1969 he was honorably discharged with the rank of captain. While serving with the marines, Smith was able to observe firsthand the military's logistics system, procurement, and delivery procedures. This rich learning experience gave him the confidence that he would be able to achieve his dream of a vast network dedicated to overnight commercial delivery. Less than two years after leaving the Marine Corps, Smith started FedEx on June 18, 1971. On the first night, fourteen jets took off with 186 packages. By 1973 FedEx was offering services to twenty-five cities. In 2012 FedEx's revenue was $427 billion, and the number of employees was more than three hundred thousand. FedEx was named by Fortune magazine as one of the top one hundred companies to work for in 2013, citing the company's choice to downsize with voluntary buyouts rather than involuntary layoffs. In March 2014 Fortune magazine ranked Smith twenty-sixth in the list of world's greatest leaders.

You Too Can Develop a Positive Attitude

- Start believing in yourself and your abilities, and develop self-confidence.

- Be an optimist, and look at all challenges and setbacks as passing phases of your life. Have faith that you will be able to overcome them successfully.

- Make positive affirmations and statements about yourself such as "I am feeling great" and "I am confident."

- Don't be afraid of failures or making mistakes. Consider your failures and mistakes as stepping-stones to success.

- Develop a pleasing personality, and be enthusiastic and cheerful in your outlook and behavior.

Eight
Leaders Are Persistent

"Nothing in the world can take the place of persistence. Talent will not; nothing is more common than unsuccessful people with talent. Genius will not; unrewarded genius is almost a proverb. Education will not; the world is full of educated derelicts. Persistence and determination alone are omnipotent." - Calvin Coolidge

"Persistence in spite of all obstacles, discouragement, and impossibilities: It is this that in all things distinguishes the strong soul from the weak." –Thomas Carlyle

"The key to successful leadership today is influence, not authority." - Kenneth Blanchard

One of the greatest qualities of leaders is persistence. Persistent people will never give up on their dreams and goals, for they know that persistence is an imperative and indispensable quality for their success. They are fully aware that when they are pursuing their goals, in spite of their hard work, commitment, and dedication, they may have to meet with failures, obstacles, barriers, hurdles, and setbacks. They also know that they may have to go through periods of frustration and disappointments. But they refuse to be discouraged by these hurdles in their path. History is replete with examples of leaders who persisted to accomplish great feats in various frontiers, including art, literature, medicine, and science.

Leaders give so much importance to persistence because they know that persistence is one great quality that can even make up or compensate for their lack of talents. President Abraham Lincoln, Henry Ford, R.H. Macy, Winston Churchill, Sam Walton, and others mentioned in this chapter proved that they were able to achieve success because of their persistence.

Common Traits of Persistent Leaders

• They keep persevering until they triumph. They know that they cannot expect to have overnight success. So instead of giving up, they recognize that if they are persistent in their efforts and keep working regardless of adversity and obstacles, sooner or later they will be able to achieve their goals.

• They refuse to be discouraged by setbacks. Even in the face of setbacks, disappointments, and challenges, they refuse to be discouraged. Instead, they bounce back every time they fail.

• They never give up what they are doing. Their motto will always be "never, ever, give up," and they will maintain a "never-say-die" attitude.

• They take guidance and advice from others when they have to make difficult or major decisions. They also emulate other successful people who have done similar things in their lives.

• They are not afraid of failure. They learn from their failures and analyze why they failed, and then incorporate the lessons of their failures into their future actions. They consider failures to be stepping-stones to success.

• They are highly committed people who can endure hardships and struggles and are determined to finish what they have started and achieve what they want. Even in the face of insurmountable problems, they will not quit.

- They are steadfast in their beliefs. They plan, practice, and prepare to face challenges, which gives them confidence.

- They visualize positive results and achieving their goals.

President Abraham Lincoln

(Sixteenth president of the United States)

President Abraham Lincoln is widely regarded as one of the greatest presidents in US history. But before becoming president, his life wasn't easy, and he had to go through a series of struggles, setbacks, and failures.

Lincoln was born on February 12, 1809, in Hardin County, Kentucky. Since he had to work constantly to support his family, his formal education was limited to an estimated total of eighteenth months—a few days or weeks at a time. However, he was a voracious reader, and he would walk for miles to borrow books from libraries. He taught himself law by reading Williams Blackstone's Commentaries on the Laws of England and other law books. After passing the bar examination in 1836, he worked as a lawyer in Springfield, Illinois, and earned a reputation as "Honest Abe."

Lincoln's life is a great illustration of the power of persistence. He experienced many failures and defeats both before and during his political career. For example, Lincoln tried opening two different stores, which both failed, leaving him with considerable debt. He also ran for and lost several posts in both state and US governments, including Illinois State Legislature, the US Senate, and vice president of the United States.

In his personal life, also Lincoln had several tragedies. In 1835 his girlfriend died, and the next year he had a nervous breakdown. Lincoln's son, Edward, died in February 1850 at the age of four due to tuberculosis. His other son, Willie, died of a fever in February 1862 at the age of twelve. The deaths of two of his four children had a profound impact on Lincoln. Lincoln also suffered from clinical depression.

In 1860 Lincoln was elected as the president of the United States, and he selected a strong cabinet composed of many of his political rivals. During his first term, Lincoln led the United States through the American Civil War and preserved the Union. He also played a historical role in abolishing of slavery. He strengthened the federal government, and modernized the economy. Lincoln's 1863 Gettysburg Address was a statement of America's dedication to the principles of nationalism, republicanism, equal rights, liberty, and democracy.

While in his second term of presidency, Lincoln was assassinated on April 14, 1865, by John Wilkes Booth at Ford's Theater in Washington, DC.

Henry Ford

(Founder of the Ford Motor Company)

Henry Ford, an American industrialist and the founder of the Ford Motor Company, was responsible for transforming the automobile from an expensive vehicle into a practical conveyance that profoundly shaped the twentieth century. But success never came easily to Ford. He suffered setbacks early in his career. His attempts to manufacture automobiles and start a company failed several times. But Ford was persistent in pursing his dream and shrugged off his critics. He put into practice his belief that "failure is simply the opportunity to begin again, this time more intelligently."

Ford was born on July 30, 1863, in Dearborn, Michigan. Even as a young boy, Ford demonstrated mechanical ability and a knack for learning by trial and error. Because of his fascination with machines, he did not want to follow his father's footsteps and become a farmer. Instead, he decided to pursue his dream, and in 1879 at the age of sixteen, he left his father's farm to become an apprentice at the Michigan Car Company, a manufacturer of railroad cars in Detroit. During the next two and half years, Ford changed jobs several times. In 1882 he returned home and operated portable steam engines used by farmers.

In 1891 Ford took up a job as an engineer for the Edison Illuminating Company, and two years later he was promoted to chief engineer. While working there, Ford built his first gasoline-powered horseless carriage, the "Quadricycle," which consisted of a light metal frame fitted with four bicycle wheels and powered by a two-cylinder, four-horsepower gasoline engine. Ford test drove it on June 4, 1896.

Ford designed and built a second vehicle in 1898. He resigned from the Edison Illuminating Company and founded the Detroit Automobile Company in August 1899. However, because the automobiles produced were of inferior quality and were too expensive, the company was not successful, and the investors lost confidence in Ford. The company was dissolved in January 1901, within one and half years.

Ford did not waste his time feeling sorry for himself. Within a few months he developed a twenty-six-horsepower vehicle. He succeeded in convincing some of the original investors in the Detroit Automobile Company to get back onboard. In November 1901 they formed the Henry Ford Company with Ford as chief engineer. Very soon things turned sour for Ford. Since the company was not doing well, a new consultant was brought in to help liquidate the company. Ford left in protest; however, the company stayed open and was renamed the Cadillac Automobile Company. Subsequently, Cadillac was bought by General Motors.

Even after two failures, Ford was not disheartened. With the help of new investors, in June 1903 the Ford Motor Company was formed with $28,000 in capital. One month after establishing the Ford Motor Company, the two-cylinder, eight-horsepower Model A was assembled. In October 1908 the Model T was introduced. The car was simple to drive, and its price was cheap at $825. Ford implemented techniques of mass production, such as the use of large production plants, standardized, interchangeable parts, and the moving assembly line. Mass production substantially cut down the time needed to produce an automobile, which in turn reduced the price. By 1918 half of all cars in America were Model Ts, and by 1927 over fifteen million Model T cars were produced, a record that stood for the next forty-five years.

Ford died on April 7, 1947, at the age of eighty-three due to cerebral hemorrhage.

R. H. Macy

(Founder of Macy's department store)

Rowland Hussey Macy experienced series of failures in his life before he became a successful businessman. It was his quality of persistence that enabled him to prevail over failures and come out triumphantly as the founder of the department store chain R. H. Macy & Co.

Macy was born on August 30, 1822, on Nantucket Island, Massachusetts. He left home at the age of fifteen to work on a whaling ship. He returned to Massachusetts after four years and worked in his father's shop for a few years. In 1844 Macy opened a needle and thread store in Boston, but in less than a year, it went bankrupt. In 1846 he opened a store selling dry goods, which also failed. After briefly working in his brother-in-law's Boston shop, Macy fled to California with his brother to take part in the 1849 gold rush. There he opened a store that sold goods to miners, but when gold ran out, the miners left, and the store was closed. With great disappointment they returned to Massachusetts, and Macy opened the first Macy's store in Haverhill in 1851 to serve the mill-industry employees of the area. That store also failed. Thus, between 1843 and 1845, Macy opened four retail dry goods stores, and they all failed. But these failures didn't deter the thirty-six-year-old Macy from pursuing his dreams. Learning from his earlier mistakes and with determination and renewed vigor, Macy moved to New York City in 1858 and established a new store named R. H. Macy Dry Goods at the corner of Sixth Avenue and 14th Street.

Macy was successful in New York. His store became well known for several innovations that transformed the retail sector. For instance, he introduced one price system, where the same item was sold to every customer at one price. He also quoted specific prices for goods in newspaper advertising. Macy's was the first store to sell products such as tea bags, Idaho baked potatoes, and colored bath towels.

Macy's employed the first in-store Santa Claus during Christmas holidays. Macy believed that women were just as capable as men, and he promoted a saleswoman, Margaret Getchell, to store manager in 1866, making her the first woman in the United States to hold an executive post in a major retail store. Another innovation was to introduce store exhibits with a theme and lighted window displays to attract customers from the street. He also offered his customers a money-back guarantee and accepted mail orders. He adopted the red star as Macy's logo, inspired by the red star tattoo on his forearm that he got while at his whaling job.

Macy died in Paris in 1877 of Bright's disease at the age of fifty-four. By that time Macy's store had grown to a chain of one hundred connected buildings and employed four hundred people.

The obituary in The New York Times praised Macy's accomplishments as follows: "His energy and enterprise in business and the strict attention he gave to every detail of it gained for him a host of staunch friends...In fact, from comparatively nothing, Macy became one of the best known and most successful merchants of the day."

Colonel Harland Sanders

(Founder of Kentucky Fried Chicken)

Colonel Harland Sanders was one of the most persistent people in the world. From Sanders's life it is abundantly clear that, more than anything, it was his persistence that paved the way for his astounding and impressive success.

Sanders was born on September 9, 1890, in Henryville, Indiana. After the death of his father when he was six years old, his mother was forced to go to work to take care of the family, and Sanders had to take care of his two younger siblings, including cooking food for them. By the age of seven, Sanders had become an expert on several local dishes, including a special chicken recipe.

Sanders left his family when he was thirteen and did several jobs, including working as a farm laborer, painter of horse carriages, streetcar conductor, soldier, blacksmith helper, and railroad fireman. Meanwhile, Sanders studied law by correspondence through the La Salle Extension University. He practiced law in Little Rock, Arkansas, for three years. His legal career ended after he had a courtroom brawl with his own client. Subsequently, Sanders worked as a laborer on the Pennsylvania Railroad, as a life insurance agent for the Prudential Life Insurance Company, a ferryboat owner, and a salesman for the Michelin Tire Company.

In 1930 Sanders took over a Shell gas station in Corbin, Kentucky, a small town on the edge of the Appalachian Mountains. In the adjacent living quarters, he served travelers unique Southern breaded-chicken dishes and other meals. Four years later he shifted to a larger gas station on the other side of the road and expanded his business to six tables. In 1936 Kentucky governor Ruby Laffoon gave him the honorary title of "Kentucky Colonel" in recognition of his contributions to the state's cuisine. In 1937 Sanders expanded his restaurant to 142 seats and added a hotel, naming it Sanders Court and Cafe. By 1940 Sanders had finalized his "secret recipe" for frying chicken in a pressure fryer that cooked chicken faster than panfrying.

In 1955 when Sanders was sixty-five, he sold his Sanders Court and Cafe after the new Interstate 75 reduced his restaurant's customer traffic. Being confident of the quality of his fried chicken, Sanders devoted himself to developing his chicken franchising business. He looked for financiers to invest in his business, but they all turned him away. After hundreds of rejections, Sanders changed his strategy and looked for people willing to make and sell his unique chicken recipe. For two years Sanders traveled across the country in his car and met with thousands of restaurant owners, hoping to develop a franchise. In two years only five restaurants had signed up. He entered into a "handshake agreement" with them, stipulating that Sanders would be given a nickel for each chicken sold in their restaurants. Over the next four years, another two hundred restaurateurs bought his franchise. By 1963 Sanders had more than six hundred KFC outlets in the United States, making the company the largest fast-food operation in the country. In 1964 Sanders sold KFC to a group of investors for $2 million. The contract included a lifetime salary for Sanders and the agreement that he would be the company's quality controller and trademark.

By 1970 KFC had three thousand outlets in forty-eight different countries. Sanders died in 1980 at the age of ninety due to leukemia, and by that time KFC had about six thousand outlets in forty-eight countries, with $2 billion sales annually. By 2013 KFC had about eighteen thousand nine hundred outlets in more than eighty-six countries with sales of $23 billion.

Sam Walton

(Founder of Walmart)

Sam Walton, founder of the Walmart retail chain, was driven by his mission "to provide a better shopping experience for everyday people living in small towns." He wanted to improve their standards of living by providing quality goods at low prices in a pleasant shopping environment. Walton's basic tenets for doing successful business included a commitment to business, sharing profits with his associates and treating them like his partners, and exceeding customers' expectations. Walton brought new approaches and technologies to retail business, and he experimented with new store formats such as Sam's Club and the Walmart Super Center.

Walton was born on March 29, 1918, in Kingfisher, Oklahoma. In 1940 he graduated with a degree in economics from the University of Missouri. After graduation Walton served as a captain in the US Army in an intelligence unit during World War II. Upon return from the army in 1945, he acquired a Ben Franklin franchise in Newport, Arkansas, using his own saving of $5000 and a loan of $20,000 from his father-in-law. Walton implemented several innovative concepts in running his business. He stocked a wide range of goods and sold them at low prices. His store was also open for longer hours than other stores in Newport. He managed to get lower prices from wholesalers and kept his profit margin small, and as a result he was able to sell larger quantities. While the store was doing $72,000 in sales when he bought it, within three years the store's sales increased to $225,000.

Walton's landlord P. K. Holmes admired the success of Walton's store, and he wanted to reclaim the store and transfer franchise rights to his son. Since Walton had no intention of selling the store, Holmes refused to renew Walton's five-year lease. Walton's persistence prevailed over the disappointment in Holmes' refusal to renew the lease. In the summer of 1950, Walton opened Walton's 5&10 in the tiny community of Bentonville; this time he insisted on a ninety-nine-year contract.

By 1960 Walton owned fifteen Ben Franklin stores, but he was not making as much profit as expected. So he planned to adopt a new strategy of discounting, cutting down prices and making up the difference through higher volumes of sales. However, the directors of the Ben Franklin Company refused to accept this strategy, so Walton decided to go on his own. By mortgaging his home and borrowing heavily, Walton opened the first Walmart in 1962 in Rogers, Arkansas, when he was forty-four. Within five years Walmart had twenty-four stores with monthly sales of over $1 million. In 1976 Walmart had 276 stores, and its sales hit more than $100 million per month. In 2013 Walmart had over eleven thousand stores in twenty-seven countries, with 2.2 million employees and a revenue of $468.65 million.

Walton was named the wealthiest man in the United States in 1985 by Forbes magazine, with an estimated worth of $2.8 billion. He was included in Time magazine's 1998 list of 100 Most Important People of the 20th Century. Walton, however, was a humble man throughout his life. He and his wife, Helen, lived in the same house in Bentonville, Arkansas, from 1959 until his death on April 5, 1992, due to bone marrow cancer.

Ralph Lauren

(American fashion designer)

Ralph Lauren has proved in his life that persistence pays. His story is one of fulfilling the American dream. Born in Bronx, New York, on October 14, 1939, he changed his last name from Lifshitz to Lauren when he was sixteen. His parents were Ashkenazi Jewish immigrants from Belarus. He attended Baruch College in Manhattan for two years and studied business.

After serving in the US Army for two years, Lauren worked briefly for Brooks Brothers as a sales assistant. In 1966 Lauren became a salesman for a tie company. While working there, Lauren was inspired to design a wide European-style necktie. The owner of the company didn't like Lauren's tie designs, and he sarcastically told Lauren, "No, the world is not ready for Ralph Lauren." Lauren felt so humiliated by this sarcastic comment that he quit his job and decided to go out on his own. Although he had little money and it was a risky venture, he started his company in a tiny space in the Empire State Building in New York.

In his new business, Lauren went around collecting rags and making them into ties. He sold those ties to small shops in New York. Gradually, sales grew, and he got his break when Neiman Marcus, the American luxury department store, bought his one hundred dozen ties.

In 1967 Lauren branded his neckties under the name Polo and began selling them at large department stores. Later, he expanded his business to a full men's wear line. Around 1970 he also released a line of women's suits tailored in a classic men's style. Lauren's business expanded rapidly in the 1980s and 1990s, and he opened boutiques in the United States and abroad. Polo went public in June 1977. Forbes magazine estimated Lauren's wealth at $7 billion as of September 2012.

From Lauren's impressive and astounding success, it

is obvious that without his employer's sarcasm and his persistent efforts to build business, none of his achievements could have happened.

Tommy Hilfiger

(Creator of the Tommy Hilfiger and Tommy clothing lines)

Tommy Hilfiger (born on March 24, 1951, in Elmira, New York) is a self-taught fashion designer. Hilfiger had to go through a series of setbacks, including being fired from a job, failed businesses, and bankruptcy. However, it was persistence that made him an immensely successful fashion designer of international acclaim.

Hilfiger started his first clothing store from the basement of his friend's house. Eventually, he opened a chain of seven boutiques that sold jeans; however, due to financial difficulties, he declared bankruptcy. Hilfiger went back to sketching new clothing designs, which helped him get a job with Jordache. Within one year he was fired from this job for unknown reasons. Hilfiger then opened a sportswear company called Twentieth Century Survival. This company was closed within one year. Despite these setbacks, however, Hilfiger didn't give up his determination to be successful, because he knew that "it takes hard work, resourcefulness, perseverance and courage to succeed."

While working as a freelance fashion designer, Hilfiger met Mohan Murjani, a businessman who was planning to launch a line of men's clothing. Murjani believed that Hilfiger was the right person to approach men's fashion in an innovative manner. He offered Hilfiger the job of overseeing a design team for a line of Coca-Cola clothing. He also let Hilfiger develop his own line of clothing. In its first year in 1984, the Coca-Cola line of clothes sold more than $100 million. For Hilfiger's signature collection, he modernized button-down shirts, and sales surpassed $5 million in the first year in 1985. By 1986 sales had increased to $16 million. By 2004 Hilfiger had five thousand four hundred employees, and his revenue had reached more than $1.8 billion. He sold his company in 2006 to Apax Partners, a private investment company. In 2010 Tommy Hilfiger Corporation was bought by Phillips Van Heusen, owner of Calvin Klein.

Hilfiger has received several awards and recognitions including the Designer of the Year Award in 1998 from the Parson School of Design in New York City, GQ magazine's International Designer of the Year in 2002, the UNESCO Support Award for his philanthropic efforts, and the Marie Curie Lifetime Achievement Award.

You Too Can Become Persistent

- Realize that as you pursue your goals, you are likely to come across challenges, obstacles, setbacks, failures, and disappointments.

- Take a firm resolution in your mind that you will not give up at any cost. In pursuit of achieving your goals, your motto should be "never, ever, give up."

- Be an optimist, and have faith that if you keep persisting and persevering, eventually you will succeed in achieving your goals and dreams.

- Focus your attention, energy, and time on finding solutions to your problems.

- Analyze the reasons for your failures, mistakes, and setbacks. Learn valuable lessons from your analysis, and incorporate these lessons into your future actions.

- Consider that your failures are stepping-stones to success.

Nine
Leaders Are Early Risers

"Early to bed and early to rise makes a man healthy, wealthy, and wise" - Benjamin Franklin

"Lose an hour in the morning, and you will be all day hunting for it" – Richard Whatley

"Outstanding leaders go out of their way to boost the self-esteem of their personnel. If people believe in themselves, it's amazing what they can accomplish." - Sam Walton

Many leaders make it a point to wake up early. Statesmen, politicians, community and spiritual leaders, writers, artists, and sportsmen as well as people from all walks of life belong to this group. Normally, these people wake up around 5:00 a.m. or even earlier. They are cognizant of the many benefits of waking up early. First, after a good night's sleep, their bodies and minds are fresh, clear, relaxed, and full of energy. Second, these early hours are peaceful and tranquil, without any distractions or interruptions. Third, they have better control of their time and can accomplish a lot. For these reasons, their early-morning hours are more productive and focused, and they are able to work with better concentration and attention.

The habit of early rising developed by people including Pope Francis, Tim Cook, and Robert Iger may convince you of the benefits you can reap by following their paths.

Common Traits of Leaders Who Wake Up Early

- They use their early-morning hours to pursue whatever they like to do. For example, depending on their interests, they spend this time reading, writing, exercising, painting, sketching, practicing music, practicing yoga, walking, biking, swimming, or working out. They are motivated to wake up early. Once they are used to getting up early, they look forward to using this block of precious time. Because they are motivated and thoroughly enjoy what they do, they don't want to waste this time. Many of them also use this time for nurturing their career, building their business, or brainstorming new ideas and new projects. They also spend time developing new hobbies or pursuing their favorite hobbies.

- To maintain the habit of waking up early, successful people keep disciplined and strict schedules for going to bed. They also eat healthy food and avoid consuming stimulants in the evenings.

Examples of Leaders Waking up Early

Pope Francis
(Reigning pope of the Catholic Church)

Born Jorge Mario Bergoglio, on December 17, 1936, Pope Francis is the pope of the Catholic Church. Born in Buenos Aires, Argentina, he was ordained as a Catholic priest in 1969, he became the archbishop of Buenos Aires in 1998, and he was created a cardinal in 2001 by Pope John Paul II. Following the resignation of Pope Benedict XVI on February 28, 2013, a papal conclave elected Bergoglio as his successor on March 13, 2013. He chose Francis as his papal name in honor of Saint Francis of Assisi. Francis is the first Jesuit pope, the first pope from the Americas, the first pope from the Southern Hemisphere, and the first non-European pope since Pope Gregory III in 741. Pope Francis has been noted for his humility and concern for the poor. He is also known for having a simpler and less formal approach to the papacy. Pope Francis has long been a stickler for setting aside enough time to pray. He gets up at 4:30 a.m. to ensure that he isn't rushed through his daily meditations.

Narendra Modi

(Prime Minister of India)

Narendra Modi was born on 17 September 1950 to a family of grocers in Mehsana district, in Gujarat, India. He became the 15th prime minister of India on May 26, 2014. Prior to that he served as the chief minister of Gujarat from 2001 to May 2014. Modi has been praised for his economic policies, which are credited with creating an environment for a high rate of economic growth in Gujarat.

Modi rises at 5 a.m. daily for yoga stretches and deep breathing, and he credits this regimen with his ability to sleep just a few hours each night.

Tim Cook

(CEO of Apple Inc.)

Timothy Donald Cook is an American business executive who succeeded Steve Jobs as the CEO of Apple on August 24, 2011. He was born on November 1, 1960 in Mobile, Alabama, United States. He earned a BS in industrial engineering from Auburn University in 1982 and an MBA from Duke University in 1988.

Cook spent 12 years in IBM's personal computer business, ultimately serving as the director of North American Fulfillment. Later, he served as COO of the computer reseller division of Intelligent Electronics, and was Vice President for Corporate Materials at Compaq for six months.

Cook gets up at 4:30 a.m. and plans his schedule during the early hours.

Robert Iger

(CEO of The Walt Disney Company)

Robert Iger is an American businessman and the chairman and CEO of The Walt Disney Company. Iger was born on February 10, 1951 in Long Island, New York. Iger completed his undergraduate studies at Ithaca College where he graduated magna cum laude with a Bachelor of Science degree in Television & Radio.

Iger has built on Disney's rich history of unforgettable storytelling with the acquisition of Pixar (2006), Marvel (2009), and Lucasfilm (2012), three of the entertainment industry's greatest storytelling companies. He has also made Disney an industry leader through its creative content offerings across new and multiple platforms.

Iger regularly gets up at 4:30 a.m., and he makes use of the early hours to plan his activities for the day.

Al Sharpton Jr.

(American Baptist minister, civil rights activist)

Alfred Charles Sharpton, Jr. is an American Baptist minister, civil rights activist, and television and radio talk show host. He was born on October 3, 1954 in the Brownsville neighborhood of Brooklyn, New York City. Sharpton graduated from Samuel J. Tilden High School in Brooklyn, and attended Brooklyn College, dropping out after two years in 1975. Former mayor of New York City Ed Koch said that Sharpton deserves the respect he enjoys among Black Americans: "He is willing to go to jail for them, and he is there when they need him." President Barack Obama said that Sharpton is "the voice of the voiceless and a champion for the downtrodden."

Sharpton wakes up around 5:00 a.m., and by 6:00 a.m. he is in the gym in his Upper West Side apartment building in New York City.

Margaret Thatcher

(Former prime minister of the United Kingdom)

Margaret Thatcher (1925–2013) was the prime minister of the United Kingdom from 1979 to 1990 and the leader of the Conservative Party from 1975 to 1990. She was the longest-serving British prime minister of the twentieth century and was the only woman to have held the office. A Soviet journalist called her the "Iron Lady," a nickname that became associated with her uncompromising politics and leadership style. As prime minister she implemented policies that have come to be known as Thatcherism. Originally a research chemist before becoming a barrister, Thatcher was an early riser, starting her day around 5:00 a.m.

Thomas Jefferson

(American Founding Father)

Thomas Jefferson (1743–1826) was an American Founding Father, the principal author of the Declaration of Independence (1776), the third president of the United States (1801–1809), and the founder of the University of Virginia. He voiced the aspirations of a new America as no other individual of his era. As a public official, historian, philosopher, and plantation owner, he served his country for over five decades.

Jefferson woke up early every day. He said, "Whether I retire to bed early or late, I rise with the sun."

You Too Can Develop the Habit of Waking Up Early

- Develop willpower and the habit of getting up early.
- To begin with, go to sleep one hour earlier than your normal bedtime so that it will be easier to wake up one hour earlier than your normal wake-up time.
- Do something you enjoy or are passionate about in the morning so you will be motivated to wake up early.
- Keep a disciplined lifestyle and a strict schedule for going to bed.
- Eat healthy food and avoid consuming stimulants in the evenings.
- Once you have developed the habit of waking up early, you can use your early-morning hours to pursue whatever you would like to do.

Ten
Leaders Pursue Excellence

"If people knew how hard I had to work to gain my mastery, it wouldn't seem wonderful at all." – Michelangelo

"The average person puts only 25% of his energy and ability into his work. The world takes off its hat to those who put in more than 50% of their capacity, and stands in its head for those few and far between souls who devote 100%." - Andrew Carnegie

"Concentrate all your thoughts on the task at hand. The sun's rays do not burn until brought to a focus." – Alexander Graham Bell

Pursuit of excellence is an integral part of leaders. They are convinced that excellence is a noble pursuit and for achieving excellence, they should do their best by putting their heart and soul on the task at hand. While they won't let anything distract them or divert their attention, they also despise mediocrity and will go the extra mile to over-deliver on their promises. They are self-disciplined, work hard, and make continual improvements on their performance.

Charlie Chaplin, Vince Lombardi, Ray Kroc, and Bill Clinton are some of the highly successful people who relentlessly pursued excellence. Their lives are truly a source of inspiration for us to pursue excellence and become successful in life.

Common Traits of Leaders Who Pursue Excellence

- They embrace excellence. They despise mediocrity and are not satisfied with work that is "just good enough." When they perform a job or a task, they always look for ways to do an excellent job that sets them apart.
- They go the extra mile. They consistently over deliver on their promises. They know that when they exceed expectations, they make themselves more valuable and indispensable. They reap the benefits, such as promotions, bonuses, pay increases, and extra compensation and recognition. They put in extra effort without compensation, feeling confident that eventually they will receive recognition and compensation for their efforts.
- They work hard. In their quest to do an outstanding job, they are willing to do ceaseless hard work. For achieving excellence, they also demonstrate perseverance, tenacity, enthusiasm, diligence, and zeal.
- They are self-disciplined. They pursue excellence with discipline, and they take full control of themselves. They plan their work properly and execute it well.
- They make continual improvements. They are highly committed to improving their character, skills, knowledge, and performance. Each day they strive to ensure they are better than the previous day in every area of their lives, including job, marriage, family, and relationships. They prepare action plans to excel in whatever they do.
- They have good control over their time. They give top priority to dealing with the most challenging situations. They don't hesitate to say "no" when they should, because they know that not saying "no" is a big time-saver when the situation demands.
- They are highly focused on whatever they do. Instead

of scattering their attention on many things, they focus completely on one thing at a time.

- They are deeply committed. They have a strong commitment and passion for their activities. They are determined to go through the ups and downs with vigor, enthusiasm, and intensity to achieve excellent results.

- They have a positive attitude. They respond to problems with a cheerful spirit. They also show courage in the face of defeat, and they won't allow an obstacle to become an excuse for not doing an excellent job.

- They visualize what they want to accomplish, and they have clear ideas on actions to be taken. They practice desired actions in their mind many times before actually performing them.

- They are confident about their potential to overcome obstacles and achieve excellence in whatever they decide to do.

- They control distractions. They do not allow distractions to interfere with the quality of their work and performance. Even in the face of distractions, they remain highly focused on their tasks.

Charlie Chaplin
(Comedic British actor)

Charlie Chaplin was one of the most pivotal stars in the history of the film industry. He was also one of the most popular comedians ever. Recognized as an icon of the silent film era, Chaplin was born on April 16, 1889, in London, England. His father, Charlie Chaplin Sr., an actor and singer, was an alcoholic who did not take care of his family. His actress mother, Hannah, did not have a regular job and was frequently committed to a mental institution. As result, Chaplin and his brother Sydney spent a lot of their childhood in a home for destitute children.

Chaplin's acting career began at the age of eight. By the age of eighteen, he had become an accomplished and popular comedian, and by the age of twenty-one, he was a star. In 1905 by the age of twenty-six, Chaplin had become one of the most recognizable superstars, earning $670,000 a year.

Chaplin was an amazing actor and director who pursued excellence relentlessly. He worked hard to improve his films on a continual basis. His determination to excel is reflected in his words, "When I am watching one of my pictures presented to an audience, I always pay close attention to what they don't laugh at. If, for example, several audiences do not laugh at a stunt I mean to be funny, I at once begin to tear that trick to pieces and try to discover what was wrong in the idea or in the execution of it. If I hear a slight ripple at something I had not expected to be funny, I ask myself why that particular thing got a laugh."

Because of his rigorous perfectionism, Chaplin took longer to complete his pictures than other filmmakers of that era. According to his friend Ivor Montagu, "nothing but perfection would be right" for Chaplin. As he financed his films, he had the freedom to strive for excellence and shoot as many takes as he wished. Very often the takes were excessive. For instance, for every finished scene in the film The Kid, there were fifty-three takes. For the film The Immigrant, a twenty-minute movie, Chaplin shot forty thousand feet of film, which is the amount used for a regular-length feature film.

Chaplin, well known for his iconic role as the loveable Tramp, was a one-man show—he was the director, actor, writer, producer, and composer. He was the master of physical comedy, with silly walks and exaggerated facial expressions. Despite his blundering on-screen persona, Chaplin was also a disciplined director with a strict work ethic and one of the most demanding men in Hollywood. It was not uncommon for Chaplin to redo one scene ten or twenty times. He walked each actor through every scene. According to Hooman Mehean, historian and author of Chaplin's Limelight and the Music Hall Tradition, "Chaplin was a perfectionist, the king of the re-take." Mehean gives the example of Chaplin having 341 takes when the actress Virginia Cherrill had to just say the words, "Flower, sir?" for the 1931 silent movie City Lights.

"He was very tough on set." said Mehean. Marlon Brando, who was a method actor and really wanted to understand what his character was feeling for his role in Chaplin's 1967 film A Countess from Hong Kong, said to Chaplin, "I don't understand my character's motivation in this scene." Chaplin replied, "Forget about motivation, just do it as I tell you to do it, that's your motivation."

Chaplin was married four times and had a total of eleven children. He died on December 25, 1977, in Switzerland.

Vince Lombardi

(American football coach)

Vince Lombardi, one of the most recognizable and successful coaches in American football, was born on June 11, 1913, in Brooklyn, New York. After graduating from Fordham University in 1937, Lombardi enrolled in Fordham Law School in 1938. He dropped out of law school after one semester and took up an assistant coaching job at St. Cecilia High School in Englewood, New Jersey, in 1939.

Lombardi worked as an assistant coach for Fordham University's varsity football team for two seasons (1947–48) and the US Military Academy at West Point for five seasons (1949–1953). In 1954 Lombardi began his National Football League (NFL) career with the New York Giants. By the third season, he turned the Giants into a championship team, defeating the Chicago Bears 47–7 for the league title in 1956.

In 1959 at the age of forty-five, Lombardi became the head coach and general manager of the Green Bay Packers. At that time the Packers were going through the worst period in their history. For the 1958 NFL season, the Packers finished with a record that left the players dispirited. Lombardi was approached by the Packers' management to take the coaching job. Having gained a reputation for his sophisticated and creative craftsmanship, Lombardi was an effective and successful head coach.

After taking over the Packers, Lombardi put his plan into action. He told the players, "I have never been on a losing team, gentlemen, and I do not intend to start now." In his pursuit of excellence, Lombardi introduced a strict training regime. He demanded absolute commitment, devotion, and dedication from his players. Lombardi immediately transformed the team in several ways, such as the way the team looked, how it played, and how it thought. He also redesigned the Packers' uniforms as well as their logo. Lombardi spent long hours studying the films of the team's games and taking appropriate actions to improve the performance of his players.

Lombardi's efforts showed immediate results. In 1959 Lombardi was named "coach of the year." In 1960 in Lombardi's second year, the Packers won the NFL Western Conference for the first time since 1944. Lombardi then coached the Packers to win their next nine postseason games. The Packers defeated the Giants for the NFL title in 1961 and 1962. Lombardi went on to compile a 105–35–6 record and never had a losing streak.

Lombardi took the Packers to three consecutive NFL championships in 1965, 1966, and 1967. In addition, in the 1966 and 1967 seasons, the Packers won the first two Super Bowls. In short, under Lombardi's coaching the Packers won six division titles, five NFL championships, and the first two Super Bowls.

In 1969 Lombardi became the head coach and general manager of the Washington Redskins. At that point in time, the Redskins were struggling. Under Lombardi's stewardship the Redskins finished their first season with their best record in fourteen years.

Lombardi died of cancer in Washington, DC, on Septemb

SATI ACHATH

Ray Kroc

(Built McDonald's into the most successful fast-food operation in the world)

Raymond Kroc's most striking quality was his pursuit of excellence. His emphasis on excellence is reflected in his famous statement, "If I had a brick for every time I've repeated the phrase Quality, Service, Cleanliness and Value, I think I'd probably be able to bridge the Atlantic Ocean with them."

Kroc was born to parents of Czech origin in Oak Park, Illinois, on October 5, 1902. By lying about his age, Kroc worked as a Red Cross ambulance driver in World War I when he was fifteen. Later he worked on several jobs, including as a paper-cup salesman, pianist, disc jockey, and multiple-mixer salesman. As a traveling milkshake machine salesman, he sold machines that made five shakes at a time, increasing restaurant efficiency. In 1954 he sold eight multiple mixers to McDonald brothers Dick and Mac McDonald, who owned McDonald's, a restaurant chain based in San Bernardino, California. Kroc was surprised by their huge order, and out of curiosity he visited their restaurant. He was impressed by the efficiency of the operation of this small, successful restaurant. Kroc observed that the brothers produced a limited menu, which allowed them to focus on quality at every step. He envisioned the tremendous potential of franchising McDonald's all over the United States. He offered to work as a franchising agent for a slice of the profits. The brothers agreed and allowed him exclusive rights to sell the McDonald's franchise.

In April 1955 Kroc opened his first McDonald's in the Chicago suburb of Des Plaines. For each franchise he sold, Kroc collected 1.9 percent of the gross sales, and he gave the McDonalds 0.5 percent. Kroc sold eighteen franchises in the first year. In 1961 he bought out the McDonalds for $2.7 million cash.

There are many examples to illustrate Kroc's pursuit of excellence. For example, to ensure that all McDonald's franchises strictly followed the "McDonald's Method," he developed a seventy-five-page manual that outlined every aspect of running a McDonald's operation. Franchise owners went to "Hamburger University" in Elk Grove and earned their degree in "Hamburgerology with a minor in French fries." His philosophy for a successful franchise was based on the principle of a three-legged stool: one leg was McDonald's, the second was the franchise, and the third was the McDonald's suppliers. He believed that the stool was only as strong as the three legs.

Kroc never stopped working for McDonald's until he died at the age of eighty-one on January 14, 1984, due to heart attack. He kept a close eye on the McDonald's near his office and phoned the manager to remind him to pick up the trash, clean his lot, and turn on the light at night.

Kroc's pursuit of excellence and unique innovation contributed to the universal success of the McDonald's brand. At the time of Kroc's death, McDonald's had seventy-five hundred outlets in thirty-one countries and was worth $8 billion, and his personal net worth was about $500 million.er 3, 1970, at the age of fifty-seven.

President Bill Clinton

(Forty-second president of the United States)

President Bill Clinton is one of the most charismatic personalities of modern times. Inaugurated at age forty-six, he was the third-youngest president and the second Democratic president since Franklin Roosevelt to be elected for a second term. Clinton, who served from 1993 to 2001, was an outstanding president who pursued excellence throughout his life.

Clinton was born William Jefferson Blythe III on August 19, 1946, in Hope, Arkansas, three months after his father died in a traffic accident. When he was four years old, his mother married Roger Clinton, of Hot Springs, Arkansas. He took his stepfather's last name when he was in high school.

The impressive results of Clinton's pursuit of excellence as president are evident on many fronts. During his administration, the United States enjoyed more peace and economic well-being than at any time in its history. The Violent Crime Control and Law Enforcement Act that he signed in 1994, a law that added one hundred thousand policemen and instituted harsher punishments for a variety of crimes, resulted in dropping crime rates in many places. In 1996 Clinton signed a law increasing the national minimum wage. In 1997 he succeeded in passing legislation forming the State Children's Health Insurance Program (SCHIP) for providing coverage to about five million children. He also sought legislation to upgrade education, to protect jobs of parents who must care for sick children, to restrict handgun sales, and to strengthen environmental rules.

Clinton's key achievements in foreign policy included presiding over the 1993 signing of the Oslo Accords between Israel and the Palestine Liberation Organization, stabilizing a war-torn Bosnia through the Dayton Peace Accords, and helping to end Serbia's ethnic cleansing of Albanians in Kosovo. Clinton left office with the highest end-of-office approval rating of any US president since

World War II.

Clinton's strive for excellence was also evident when he was the governor of Arkansas for five terms, serving from 1979 to 1981 and from 1983 to 1992. He succeeded in reforming the education system, transforming it from the worst in the nation into one of the best. He helped transform Arkansas's economy, removed sales tax from medications for senior citizens, and increased the home property-tax exemption.

Clinton also excelled in academics and extracurricular activities. He was a stellar student at Hot Springs High School in Arkansas, and he attended Georgetown University in Washington, DC, on a scholarship and received a bachelor of science in foreign service in 1968. After graduating from Georgetown, Clinton won a highly prestigious Rhodes Scholarship to study for two years at Oxford University. After Oxford in 1973 he earned a JD from Yale Law School. All along he also excelled in playing saxophone, and at one point he even considered becoming a professional musician.

Clinton continued his pursuit of excellence in his post presidency life. The William J. Clinton Foundation was founded in 2001 to address issues of global importance. This foundation includes several initiatives. For example, the Clinton Health Access Initiative (CHAI) is a global health organization committed to strengthening integrated health systems in the developing world and expanding access to care and treatment for HIV and AIDS, malaria, and tuberculosis. The Clinton Global Initiative (CGI) is a nonpartisan organization that convenes global leaders to devise and implement innovative solutions to the world's most pressing problems. Each year CGI hosts an annual meeting in September, scheduled to coincide with the UN General Assembly. The Clinton Climate Initiative (CCI) aims at "fighting against climate change in practical, measurable, and significant ways." CCI is working with forty of the world's largest cities to reduce their greenhouse gas emissions through a variety of large-scale programs.

Ratan Tata

(Indian industrialist and businessman)

Ratan Tata had many excellent achievements to his credit during his twenty-one-year tenure (1991 to 2012) as the chairman of Tata Sons, the holding company of the Tata Group, which is India's oldest and best-known conglomerate.

Tata was born on December 28, 1937, into an old Parsi family in Mumbai. After graduating from Cornell University with a BSc in architecture and structural engineering, he joined the Tata Group in December 1962. In his first assignment he worked on the floor along with blue-collar employees, shoveling limestone and handling blast finances.

Tata's pursuit of excellence was first demonstrated in 1971 when he was appointed the director in charge of the National Radio and Electronics Company Limited (NALCO), a company that was in dire financial difficultly. To improve NALCO's financial situation, Tata suggested the company management change its strategy by investing in high-technology products rather than in consumer electronics. Between 1972 and 1975, NALCO's financial conditions improved. Likewise, in 1977 he took charge of Empress Mills, a struggling unit of the Tata Group, and managed to turn it around and even declare a dividend.

In 1991 Tata succeeded J. R. D. Tata as the chairman of the Tata Group. He reformed the company by pushing out the old guard and ushering in younger managers. Tata very successfully reshaped the fortunes of the Tata Group and made it the company with the largest market capitalization of any business on the Indian Stock Market.

Another of Tata's excellent achievements was designing and developing India's first indigenous car, the Indica, which has emerged as one of the strongest brands in India.

In 2007 Tata Steel successfully acquired Corus Group, an Anglo-Dutch steel and aluminum producer. With the merger Tata steel became the fifth-largest steel-producing entity in the world. In 2008 Tata Motors bought Jaguar and Land Rover from the Ford Motor Company for $2.3 billion, and it became the first time an Indian automaker bought brands from a US automaker.

In 2008 Tata's dream of manufacturing the world's cheapest car was fulfilled by launching the Tata Nano, a city car designed to lure India's burgeoning middle classes, who generally ride motorcycles. The purchase price of the Nano was brought down by dispensing with most nonessential features and reducing the amount of steel used in its construction.

The government of India honored Tata with its second-highest civilian award, the Padma Vibhushan, in 2008. He has honorary doctorates from several universities in India and abroad, including Ohio State University and the Asian Institute of Technology in Bangkok, Thailand. Tata has also completed the Advanced Management Program from Harvard Business School.

You Too Can Pursue Excellence

- Don't be satisfied with mediocrity. Instead, seek excellence in whatever you do, and be determined to do your best.

- Go the extra mile by doing more than is required, and set high standards for your work and actions that go beyond others' expectations.

- Be willing to work relentlessly and demonstrate perseverance, tenacity, enthusiasm, and zeal as you work.

- Be self-disciplined—plan your work properly, and execute it well.

- Be committed to making continual improvements in your character, skills, knowledge, and performance. Each day, try to do your work better than the previous day.

- Excel in time management, and give top priority to the most challenging situations.

- Focus completely on one thing at a time. Don't allow distractions to interfere with the quality of your work.

Leadership Traits
Winning Strategies of 50 World Class Leaders